Temagami

Temagami

Michael Barnes

THE PHOTOGRAPHERS

Lynne Birnie   Gary McGuffin   Andy Stevens

Stoddart

A BOSTON MILLS PRESS BOOK

This is for Lynne Birnie, who introduced
me to Lake Temagami, and for all those who
love that wilderness country

Canadian Cataloguing in Publication Data

Barnes, Michael, 1934-
Temagami
Includes bibliographical references.
ISBN 1–55046–031–5

1. Temagami, Lake, Region (Ont.).
2. Temagami Lake , Region (Ont.) – History.
3. Temagami, Lake, Region (Ont.) – Guidebooks. I. Title.

FC3095.T44B37 1992   971.3'147   C92-093916-3
F1059. T44B37 1992

© 1992 Michael Barnes
Design and Typography by
Kinetics Design & Illustration
Printed in Canada

First published in 1992 by
Stoddart Publishing Co., Ltd.,
34 Lesmill Road, Toronto,
Canada, M3B 2T6

A BOSTON MILLS PRESS BOOK
132 Main Street, Erin, Ontario,
N0B 1T0   519-833-2407

The publisher gratefully acknowledges the support of
the Canada Council, the Ontario Arts Council and
the Ontario Publishing Centre in the development of
writing and publishing in Canada.

Front cover photos:
Andy Stevens: Pine Needles
Gary McGuffin: Canoeists

Back cover photo:
Lynne Birnie

Page 1 photo:
Andy Stevens

Page 3 photo:
Andy Stevens

Contents

Andy Stevens

Acknowledgements

AS in every work where information comes from many sources, the writer owes various debts. Lynne Birnie, who took many of the photographs that grace this book, generously offered hospitality and introduced me to the lake and to some of its people, many of whom kindly took the time to write about their experiences for me. Al Reid of the Temagami Chamber of Commerce paved the way, and support was given by other business people: Ken Richardson, George Hendrickson, and Bob Gareh, as well as Doug and Mary Adams, who offered a bed at Northland Paradise Lodge. Barbara Twain from the Teme-Augama Anishnabai gave me a welcome from the band.

Elinor Armstrong of New Liskeard flew me over Maple Mountain and Lady Evelyn Lake, and George Bishop and Darren Gareh piloted me in Lakeland Airways aircraft over Lake Temagami. Verdun Pacey took me on his boat along the North-West Arm. His brother Lorne and sister-in-law Verla shared photographs, as did Jerry Burrows, Jack L. Goodman, Bill Crofut, Thor Conway, and others too numerous to mention here but whose names appear beside their photographs in the book. Peter Cliff copied old photographs for me. Also, special thanks to Temagami artists Helen Hall and the late Pat Schroeder and to Hap Wilson who made valuable contributions.

Brian Moulder talked to me of MNR plans for the forest. Al Hyde, Finlayson Point Provincial Park Superintendent, opened up the museum, and Tim Gooderham made Temagami Lake Association archives available and explained the organization's current concerns.

Temagami librarian Elspeth McCormack loaned reference material, and more was provided by Joyce Allick of Teck Centennial Library in Kirkland Lake. Fred Reimers donated a book on Keewaydin.

Finally, there is the ever-present fear that some kind person who contributed to this book has been forgotten in these brief remarks. I hope it is not so, but if it is, accept my apologies, and know that you are appreciated none the less.

Michael Barnes

Introduction

ONLY five hours' drive from Canada's largest urban centre is a huge wilderness area, sparsely populated and largely unknown. Although Highway 11, one of the two main provincial routes, bisects this area, it has not been widely explored, other than by local property owners, as there are few secondary highways, and travel through the skein of lakes that covers much of the landscape requires the use of a boat or a canoe. This is Temagami.

Temagami lies north of North Bay, most of it in the northern half of the Nipissing District, although a portion extends into the southern half of the Timiskaming District. The area is dominated by water: Lake Temagami, countless smaller lakes, and the watersheds of three great rivers — the Sturgeon, the Montreal, and the Ottawa. Muskoka, Algonquin Park, and Quetico Park are Ontario's most popular forest areas; Temagami, although much larger than any of them, receives only a fraction of the annual visitors they each receive. This is especially surprising when one learns that within Temagami lie Ishpatina Ridge, the highest point in the province; one of the largest stands of old-growth pine left in eastern Canada; a lake so big that there is no one point where it can be centrally viewed; a great forest preserve; and that the area has provided the setting for several feature films. In addition, Grey Owl, the famous writer on wildlife and conservation, spent a considerable part of his life here.

This vast chunk of Canadian Shield was opened up at the turn of the century by the Temiskaming & Northern Ontario Railway, but did not experience a major influx of tourists at the time. Today, Temagami offers a unique insight into recreational resource management and aboriginal rights. Temagami has found itself the subject of news broadcasts in recent years and has been adopted by several opposing advocacy groups. None of these will find their causes espoused by the text of this book, although their views are summarized. Conclusions drawn will be those of the reader, not the author.

Setting the Scene

NORTHERN Ontario, a huge lonely land, covers the greater part of the province of Ontario and roughly one-tenth of Canada. Two distinct regions lie within it. The greater, to the south, lies on the Precambrian rocks of the Canadian Shield. The more northerly area, bordering James Bay and Hudson Bay, lies above much younger rocks. The southern portion contains rich mineral deposits; the lowlands below the bays have only lignite and commercial clays. Both regions generally have shallow soils except in areas where the land was once covered by vast inland seas.

The northern half of Ontario is dominated by water. From a height of land that wends its way in haphazard fashion across the north, great rivers flow — mainly northward. Only The Sturgeon and Ottawa flow south out of this network of lakes, streams, and muskeg. The Missinaibi, Kapuskasing, Groundhog, Mattagami, Fredrickhouse, and Abitibi all flow toward the northern lowlands. Five large lakes stand out on this axis. Close to James Bay is Lake Kesagami. Further south, Lake Abitibi straddles the Ontario–Quebec border, and Lake Timiskaming separates the same provinces for about 100 kilometres. West of this long lake is Lake Temagami, and just to the south Lake Nipissing sits on the historic fur-trade route between the Ottawa River and Georgian Bay.

The Temagami area covers about 12,000 square kilo-

Temagami Harbour in 1930. J. R. Stevens

metres from Elk Lake in the north, where the Montreal River broadens on its way south, to River Valley, west of North Bay at the confluence of the Sturgeon and Temagami rivers, and from Lake Timiskaming and the Ottawa River in the east, westward to the Sturgeon River. In the middle sits Lake Temagami.

Lake Temagami was once described as looking like a flower, with Bear Island as its centre. The six "petals" of this lake cover 20,210 hectares, and there are 1,259 islands, the largest being Temagami Island, followed

*The view from
Maple Mountain.*
Andy Stevens

Temagami harbour is still a busy spot.

by adjacent Bear Island. There is a 50-kilometre span from Baie Jeanne in the south to the north end of Whitefish Bay, yet at no point is this great lake wider than 8 kilometres. Estimates of the shoreline length vary from 512 to 616 kilometres. The total island shoreline is perhaps another 340 kilometres.

An old portage once connected Lake Temagami with Snake Lake, crossing the present Highway 11 and the Ontario Northland Railway tracks. The trail sat squarely between two great water systems. A pail of water thrown in one direction would flow into Caribou Lake, down through Little Sucker Creek to Inlet Bay on Lake Temagami. The water would pass down the North-East Arm, past Temagami Island, on down the South Arm, and exit the lake via the Temagami River to the Sturgeon River. Next stop would be Lake Nipissing and on

through the French River to Georgian Bay on Lake Huron, and via the lake system to the St. Lawrence River. A pail of water thrown in the other direction would run through Snake Lake and on to White Bear Lake and Rabbit Lake. From there it would reach the Matabitchewan River, the Montreal River, and Lake Timiskaming. The flow would proceed down the Ottawa River, finally entering the St. Lawrence River at Montreal. With some special Canadian luck here, a few drops might unite with water from the other pail.

Temagami country is a rocky upland plain with a shallow soil covering. The large lakes have many sandy beaches and rugged cliffs are common. This is a border zone between the great boreal forests to the north and the Great Lakes–St. Lawrence forest system to the south. Trees here are a mix of northern evergreens and hardwoods, and pine is king. White and red pines tower on rocky shores and ridges while jack pine flourishes on burned-over areas. White and black spruce and balsam fir are plentiful. Northern hardwoods such as aspen and white birch may be found adjacent to southern hardwoods like yellow birch and maple on more protected sites. There are wetland communities — scrublands, marshes, floating bogs, and black spruce bogs.

Moving ice shaped the surface of most of northern Ontario and Quebec. Four great glacial movements ebbed and flowed across this land, the last being about 11,000 years ago. The movement of great ice sheets scoured the earth, depressing the surface in some places and raising it in others. Lake Timiskaming was formed by one deep gouge left in a glacial wake. As for Lake Temagami, the great moving sheet of ice created a different waterway. Instead of forming six lakes, some caprice of nature left behind one large lake with six long, narrow strands. When the glaciers finally receded, Lake Ojibway-Barlow, a huge lake close in size to the present Great Lakes, covered much of the north. It eventually filtered away, leaving behind a gift of fertile alluvial deposits, the basis of the Clay Belts and the rich farmlands around Englehart, Earlton, and New Liskeard.

The lands around Temagami were not so fortunate. Here the bedrock was wave-washed, leaving only a thin accumulation of soil.

Native people have lived in this region for about 5,000 years. Today, about a hundred Temagami Indians live on Bear Island in winter, a number swelled by perhaps 50 more in summer. Europeans appeared in the area during the seventeenth century, but to most of them it was no more than a place to rest en route to somewhere else. White settlement did not come to Temagami until the middle of the nineteenth century. Both natives and newcomers found the area rich in wildlife — bear, moose, timber wolf, snowshoe hare, lynx, marten, fisher, and many birds.

The names of the lakes and the rivers underwent numerous spelling changes. The original Indian name for Timiskaming, meaning *deep water*, for example, was first written in French, *Témiscamingue*, and then anglicized. *Temagami* changed in the same fashion. Grey Owl noted in 1936 that "the word is Ojibway Indian derived from 'Temea' meaning 'deep' and 'Gaming' meaning 'the Lake' in particular, not a lake in the general sense. "Temeagaming' meaning 'deep-at-the-shore' is probably the original word slurred to 'Temagaming.'" •

A rainy-day break.

Lynne Birnie

The stream between Gull Lake and Lake Temagami.
Lynne Birnie

Temagami Tour

HIGHWAY 11 begins at Lake Ontario in Toronto, where it is called Yonge Street. It heads north and northwest for what feels like forever before it veers slightly south and joins U.S. 11 across the Ontario–Minnesota border at Baudette. It is an enormously long highway — nearly 2,000 kilometres — and it is the highway the traveller must take to get to Temagami.

Four hours up Highway 11 from Toronto is North Bay. Here the highway turns sharply north and passes through the great escarpment which for many years was a barrier to both road and rail development. The terrain is mixed bush and rock scattered with lakes and rivers and dotted here and there with signs warning of "Night Danger." This refers to moose. The great beasts sometimes venture out of the trees and onto the road to escape flies in summer. In confrontation with cars, usually neither party emerges unscathed.

It is here that motorists will get their first sightings of the great red and white pines. These aristocrats of the forest thrust high above the surrounding trees, their foliage sculptured by the prevailing winds. The wonder is that these handsome giants often seem to rise out of solid rock with little soil support.

From North Bay to the town of Temagami is about an hour's drive. About halfway between the two lies the

Prior to 1935 the Ferguson Highway looped around Lowell Lake.

Ann Swanson

Marten River Provincial Park and the south boundary of the Temagami Forest Reserve. Marten River Park has a particularly nice drawing card, a restored lumber camp. Loggers cut the pines here early in the century and their camp has been restored to provide a fascinating look at area history. This is one of several museums in the region.

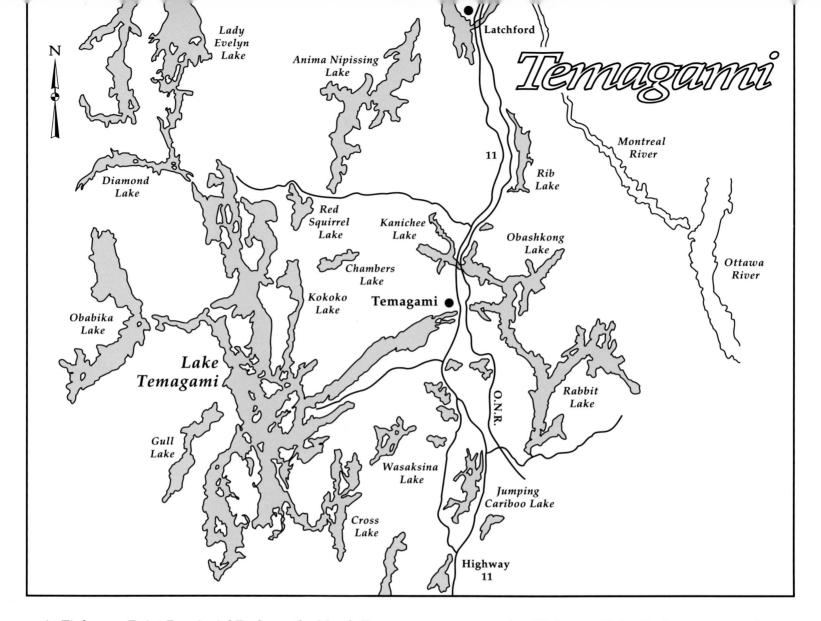

At Finlayson Point Provincial Park, on the North-East Arm of the lake, just south of the town, there is a small museum chock-full of material relating to the lake, boating, logging, trapping, Grey Owl, and the area's wildlife. Together with the sheltered dock, the sandy beach, 114 campsites nestled amongst 200-year-old white pines, and clearly marked hiking routes, this museum makes Finlayson Point Park a very popular holiday spot.

With a logging museum and a trapping museum, naturally you would expect that there would be a mining museum somewhere in the region. Indeed there is, but you won't find it until you have already visited Temagami and are headed north. The town of Cobalt is almost a museum in itself. Known as the Silver Town,

Cobalt has its official mining museum in a modest storefront building. The museum is devoted to silver mining and to the characters that made Cobalt the cradle of Canadian mining, but it also issues a pamphlet giving directions for the Silver Trail, a self-guided tour highlighting the silver rush. Following directions, you wander around the town, entranced by street signs in the form of claim posts, a former store built around a mineshaft, and numerous actual mines. The historic railway station, where piles of silver bars were left unattended in the early days, is now being refurbished to house yet another private museum, this one relating to Canada at war.

In Haileybury, just north of Cobalt, there is a fire museum commemorating the great forest fire of 1922 which almost completely destroyed the town and devastated the surrounding area.

It may be that you have arrived in Temagami to experience some boating on the great lake. You're certainly not alone. If you have brought your own boat you would

be well-advised to obtain some helpful publications available at Ministry of Natural Resources locations or at shops and trading posts in Temagami. There are many shoals in Lake Temagami and such publications as *Canoeing in Ontario* or the Ministry of Natural Resources' map *Islands in Lake Temagami* will be invaluable. One free pamphlet, *Experience Temagami*, contains a map by Hap Wilson which is an excellent guide to navigation and to campsites on the lake. Hap Wilson, with his wife Trudy, for a considerable time ran the Smoothwater Wilderness Centre on James Lake, just north of Lake Temagami and on the borders of the Nipissing and Temiskaming districts. Hap did a book for the ministry called *Temagami Canoe Routes*, which not only details 13 access points to canoe routes, it describes the trips in detail and gives much helpful technical information, including lists of equipment needed, right down to the complete food list for a week.

Hap only supports no-trace canoeing. In other words, all garbage is packed out of the wilderness and no trip he has sponsored has left behind any scars upon the land. He has taken both regular and whitewater canoeing trips, as well as photographic excursions, mountain biking, and hiking. He suggests canoeing through the Lady Evelyn–Smoothwater Provincial Park, which has Ontario's highest high point, Ishpatina Ridge, and Maple Mountain. Lady Evelyn Lake is one of the most impressive in the North, with blue-green water covering a sandy bottom. For Hap Wilson, "Temagami is the pine tree, the loon, and clear water all combined in a roadless area. Remove any one of these features and you remove the special character of the land."

South of Lake Temagami on Highway 11 is the Lake Temagami Access Road, a winding 15-kilometre gravel road that ends in a loop and a large parking lot at the lakeside. Ninety-two percent of all access to the lake is via this road. There is a launching ramp and a dock here, and boats of all sizes jostle at their moorings. Set

*Ready to head out
into Lake Temagami.*
Andy Stevens

*Whitewater kayaking is
one way in which poeple can
experience Temagami.*
Gary McGuffin

back from the dock is a large bulletin board which has news of lake events. There is a shed to shelter people waiting for friends to pick them up or for a water taxi. Depending on the time of day, one might see any of the service vessels which ply the lake: barges carrying fuel, the hydro service unit, perhaps a former landing craft carrying a bulldozer for excavation work or lumber for a new building.

Lake Temagami reveals little about itself at this access point. The view is shielded by islands. The best way to be introduced to the lake is with a short boat trip — the water taxi operators will be happy to oblige, but reserve ahead. A good route for a first-time visitor might be around the two largest islands; north for about 2 kilo-metres between Temagami Island and the mainland, and then left around the island and south again for another

2 kilometres to the dock at Bear Island. The approach to the government dock is the same as that taken by fur-trade canoes more than a century ago.

Alas, the Bear Island Trading Post burned down in the spring of 1990. It had been the former Hudson's Bay Company store and had boasted a broad verandah where old-timers sat to watch the world go by. Long-time resident Butch Turner can recall a time in the late 1930s when he stood here next to a pile of furs as tall as he was.

From Bear Island the route back to the Access Road via the southern tip of Temagami Island is marked by several islands. You will pass Camp Wabikon and the site of the first Hudson's Bay Company post. There is also an old cemetery with headstones dating from the 1880s. The graves, some still fenced with neat pickets, are fast being covered in a tangle of brush and small trees.

Another good way to see more of the lake would be to contact Bob Gareh of Lakeland Airways. Lakeland offers tour flights which allow a view of Ojibwa ceremonial sites such as Conjuring Rock on Lake Obabika or places where vision quests were performed, such as High Rock Island or Devil Mountain. A hop to the Hub and back will give a good impression of the topography of the lake.

Back on the road for the few kilometres from the Access Road to the town, you round a curve and are presented with a striking vista of Temagami. Portage Bay, once on the main canoe route between Lakes Temagami and Timiskaming, is one of the jewels of northern Ontario. In any season it is alive with colour and movement. The bay is spotted with islands, and the combination of sun, water, and sky, or — just as vivid — winter ice and snow, is always beautiful. On any day it is not uncommon to see four modes of travel simultaneously along this bay. The railway runs parallel to the road, and there can be trains, cars, boats, and float planes all in the same view.

Once in town, perhaps fortified with a bite to eat at Marg's Restaurant or the Busy Bee, a walk around the

Andy Stevens

The Temagami Canoe Company.

docks gives a good view of Temagami's waterfront. This spot has undergone many changes over the years. The former boathouse sheds have gone and in their place there is a new marina. A new municipal building and a cultural centre with library and theatre overlook the lake. Further along is the Lakeland Airways base with the Three Buoys houseboat dock, the regional office of the Ministry of Natural Resources, and the Leisure Islands houseboat location at the end of the road.

On the other side of this bay road is the Temagami Canoe Company. The building looks old and worn, as do the canoes outside it. They are in for repair. Inside the old building the Kilbridge family make some of the finest canvas-and-cedar-strip canoes on the continent. Sixteen-footers edged with brass, they weigh in at 34 kilograms, a decent load for one person. With gleaming cedar ribs and planks, white-ash gunwales, and canvas fitted, filled, sanded, and painted, these canoes are poetry in motion in the water. A visitor to the factory is often so captivated that another order results. But the purchasers of one of these approximately $2,000 hand-built canoes must be patient — each one takes three weeks to build.

If your financial situation doesn't stretch to the purchase of your own canoe you can always contact an outfitter like Bob Groves of Ogama Outfitters. In winter, Bob offers a novel vacation experience: he has researched the old winter mail route that was done by dog team, the one Grey Owl did when he had the job of winter postman, and he and his dogs escort parties of tourists who want to try wintertime bush travel.

Interior of the Temagami Canoe Company.

A major resort complex has been approved for Caribou Mountain, outside the town of Temagami. The development will have a ski hill, sports complex, golf course, hotel, and Canadian native centre. Current plans for an airport will make such development an attractive prospect for the town on the edge of Lake Temagami. In the meantime there are the boaters and the tourists and the work they bring in. Jerry Burrows, for instance, runs a large fishing boat, *The Ketch*, taking fishing enthusiasts out for charter trips. Jerry's shore lunches are highly popular. Lake Temagami has record-size fish; a lake trout weighing more than 16 kilograms was taken in 1977. That would have been a worthy competitor for the annual fall Lions Lake Trout Derby.

Latchford is the next sizeable town north of Tema-gami before you reach Cobalt. Just north of Latchford is one of the North's greatest surprises — the Highway Book Shop. It comes as a bit of a shock, indeed, to find a large, full-service bookshop on the side of a lonely highway. The owners keep all categories of books in stock, along with great bargains in remainders. Not only that, but the Highway Book Shop does its own publishing. *Backhouses of the North* has long been one of their bestsellers. It must strike a responsive chord in the hearts of many northerners who have more than a passing acquaintance with a backyard biffy.

Since the days of the Group of Seven, the colours and shapes of all the seasons in northern Ontario have called out to artists. Today, the area around Temagami is home to many artists and craftspeople. Helen Hall is one. South of the Access Road just off the highway is Lowell Lake, and here Helen has the Loft Gallery, a

A successful fly-in fishing trip.   Bob Gareh

barn-like building next to her home, where she creates and sells paintings of local scenery and birds — chickadees, loons, and the like.

Down the South-West Arm of the lake lives Terry O'Sullivan. Terry, a slender figure with a neat beard, is a sculptor as well as a painter. He is also a dedicated member of the Temagami Lakes Association and annually donates his work to be sold at the Association's sale in August. His commissioned carvings grace private homes and businesses across the country.

The Owl's Nest is a gallery in Temagami located in a brick house which used to be home to priests. It is run by Hugh Mackenzie and Wally Irvine. They also have a gallery on Bear Island. Hugh, a contemporary of famous Ojibwa artist Benjamin Chee Chee, is a popular painter. Wally also paints, but is better known for his wood sculptures. One of his larger pieces is on view on the main street of Temagami.

The Temagami area is rich in things to do and see, but it can also serve as a jumping-off spot for further excursions. Quebec is just on the other side of Lake Temiskaming, farther north are Elk Lake, Gogama, and the beautifully named Shining Tree. Perhaps you might decide to head for Cochrane, home of the famous Polar Bear Express. Or you might just stay in the Temagami region, where there's always something else to do.   •

Jerry Burrows cooks
another great shore lunch.
Lynne Birnie

Through the Past

THE first people in the Temagami region appeared in what archaeologists call the Archaic Period, from 5,000 B.C. to 400 B.C. These earliest people's lives followed the seasons and the land. In the fall, they camped by the waterways to harvest migrating wildfowl. They moved inland in winter to trap and hunt, and in spring they returned to the water to fish. Fish were caught with bait and traps rather than nets and harpoons. As the days lengthened into summer, the families gathered berries and roots and they socialized. Dugout canoes were the mode of lake travel, the bow was the main hunting weapon, and native copper was a boon to their existence. This easily worked metal provided axes, spears, even jewellery. Gradually these people spread out and traded with others to the south.

The Indians' lives gradually became more comfortable and more sophisticated. During the Middle Woodland Period, from 400 B.C. to 800 A.D., seine-net fishing ensured food stocks. Pottery provided food bowls and cooking utensils. In the Late Woodland Period, from 800 A.D. to 1600 A.D., permanent campsites were developed and gill-netting was introduced. The people began experimenting with rock painting, and religious ceremonies became common.

Archaeologists have barely scraped the surface of the land in examining the years of aboriginal life in

Pictographs created by early Temagami Ojibwa. Julie Matey Conway

Temagami before the coming of Europeans. Promising excavation sites are found on terraces near sandy beaches as well as on river and lake banks, sheltered bays, points, and islands. Thor Conway, an archaeologist with the Ministry of Culture and Communications, finds evidence of early habitation at almost any well-used portage. At Sand Point on the West Arm of Lake Temagami the diligent searcher can find remains of several temporary Indian camps. Artifacts in this area, dating to the fifteenth century, include arrowheads, pot shards, and tools.

Lake Temagami was not on the great fur-trade routes, and consequently the Indians had to travel to sell their furs and fish. In 1620 Champlain, who was at Lake Nipissing, referred in his journals to the people who hunt and fish to the north. Between 1650 and 1661 marauding Iroquois made several forays into Temagami, cutting off Temagami Indian trade ventures to the south. The Hudson's Bay Company built a fort at Moose Factory in 1673 and the French *Compagnie du Nord* began trading

nearby six years later. Temagami Indians thus began trading north from Lake Timiskaming, eventually travelling much farther north and meeting the James Bay Cree. In 1683 a Sieur d'Argenteuil received a French charter giving him trading rights to all of Lake Timiskaming. Naturally, conflict followed between the French and the English, but somehow the Temagamis escaped the tensions that racked the two trading powers.

The European trade caused the natives to rely more on imported goods and less on items of their own manufacture, especially after the Hudson's Bay Company changed its long-standing policy and began to take trade

The arrival of the railway necessitated much land clearing.

A Temagami Indian campfire ring at Obabika Lake dates from about 1500.   Julie Matey Conway

inland. Following the merger in 1821 between the Hudson's Bay Company and the North West Company, the new governor, Sir George Simpson, decided to increase competition with rivals such as the American Fur Company of Sault Ste. Marie. The American Fur Company had a small post on Lake Temagami. Simpson's resolve was strengthened when independent traders from Penetanguishene also set up in business on that lake. In 1834 Samuel Harris, one of those independents, was hired by the Hudson's Bay Company to set up a small trading post on the south side of Temagami Island.

The Temagami Indians did not restrict their trade to the new post, for they still liked the variety of trade to the south, and the post at Lake Timiskaming was much larger with more opportunities for social contact. There was an Oblate mission across the Narrows, south of present-day Haileybury, and the teaching of the Oblates interested the Indian people.

The Temagami Island post was only occupied intermittently for several years, as the Hudson's Bay Company had difficulty keeping staff in such places. Young men were leaving the United Kingdom in a

An old ladder between Lake Temagami and Link Lake.
Andy Stevens

wave of immigration to Australia and elsewhere; for those already in Canada the new railway boom offered high wages and less isolation than life in the fur trade. James Hackland, manager of the post in 1857, wrote in his diary that "of all the places I have been exposed to since I joined the Hudson Bay service, this is the most wretched." The Temagami Island post did not have a trade monopoly anyway, so it never figured prominently in Company plans.

A post was established at Fort Matachewan in 1865, but neither it nor the post at Temagami were ever more

Promotional pictures lured adventuresome OA A6286 S8125
tourists to Temagami at the turn of the century.

than sub-posts of the one at Timiskaming. Business at this time was coming not only from trappers but from surveyors, prospectors, and those who were exploring the land. Company buildings thus began to look more like general stores than fur-trade posts. By Confederation the present location of Temagami village was marked by a couple of cabins. The post on Temagami Island had never been conveniently situated, being at the bottom of a steep hill, so in 1876 it was moved to the present location on Bear Island. The only signs of the old post today are the remains of a root cellar and, up on the hillside, a small, practically overgrown cemetery.

The new Company property on Bear Island included a house, store, provision store, and a kitchen. There was a small garden with old fish nets from Timiskaming used to protect the produce from chickens. For a while the manager kept a horse and some cattle. The Hudson's Bay Company tried hard to keep customers loyal to the Temagami post. On New Year's Day 1879, for example, after an all-night dance, they provided a feast for the

The Temagami train station in 1910. J. R. Stevens

The bridge over Eagle River at Camp Wanapitei.

Temagami Indians which included 40.8 kilograms of flour, 13.5 kilograms of pork, 1 kilogram of tea, 3 kilograms of sugar, 2.75 kilograms of raisins, 2 kilograms of butter, and 1 kilogram of tobacco. Competition was strong, however. An independent trader distributed at the same time $60 worth of cakes and "other things" from Toronto.

The pace of development quickened in the last decade of the nineteenth century thanks to prospecting, government survey work, and the colonization movement, and

in 1894 C.C. Farr, the founder of Haileybury, correctly predicted Temagami's future as a tourist area. "It is not, nor will it be, a settlers' paradise; but summer tourists will rejoice in it and be glad, for a greater land than Muskoka is there. Thirteen hundred islands studded in an immense lake where water is as clear as crystal and abounding in fish, will make such a resort for city-choked, sun-scorched, dust-laden tourists as Canada never saw before. When this lake is opened up for the public, nearly every man of leisure can become, for a

Workers from many countries built the railway north to Temagami in 1903.

few months of the year, an inhabitant of his own island, an amateur Robinson Crusoe."

By this time, a few buildings were marking the site of the village of Temagami, and a little to the north, Father Charles Paradis had founded a camp that he hoped to turn into a settlement. Though the settlement never materialized he did run his camp as a home for French-Canadian orphans. It is to be hoped that the orphans enjoyed life at the camp, as the only way they could leave was by canoe. In fact, until the arrival of the railway, canoe was the only way supplies and mail reached Temagami.

Construction of the Temiskaming & Northern Ontario (later to become the Ontario Northland) Railway north from North Bay didn't begin until 1902. No private-enterprise builders could be found and so the province built the line itself. The rocky terrain offered construction challenges equal to those of the more

publicized CPR route along Lake Superior. The line reached Temagami in 1904, and by 1909 the station had occupied two different locations. The present elegant stone building used to have a garden with the town's name picked out in flowers and a separate restaurant building. With the discovery of silver at Cobalt in 1905, rail service dramatically improved, and the introduction of the special "Cobalt Flyer" meant that tourists could visit Temagami in Pullman-car comfort.

It was the railway that laid out the townsite and built the first log school in 1907. Church services were held only in summer until 1911, when an Anglican minister became the first year-round clergy. During this time, the Hudson's Bay store on Lake Timiskaming closed, leaving only the Matachewan and Temagami stores.

Soon after this, the First World War dried up the tourist traffic to Temagami. It would not return until after 1918, but it returned with a vengeance — it was not uncommon to see up to 300 people on the station platform at train time. The post-war travellers were a different lot from the pre-war ones, however. Then tourists had come mainly from the wealthy classes. Now Temagami became host to energetic young loners seeking adventure in the wild, expressing the desire to get back to life in its basic form. These were the first of the canoe contingent, intrepid trippers who always looked upon Temagami as a special place.

The 1920s brought a road to Temagami. While the most comfortable way to travel was still by train, a crooked, hilly single-lane road was gradually opened up from North Bay. Still barely more than a track, it was officially opened in July 1927. A good trip from North Bay took at least two hours. The road necessitated the opening of a garage in the village, and eventually — in 1933 — it also brought Temagami's first year-round OPP officer.

The 1930s were the Depression years, and there was a vast gap between those with jobs and those without, those with money and those without. Lucille Ball and Bob Hope had visited Bear Island in 1928, and James Stewart was a 1934 guest at Camp Adanac. There were tourists in the summer, and there was some work available on the railway. The coal chute and water tower had to be serviced, and there was a section crew, station staff, and telegraphists. But for many, government road work was the only source of employment. The road from Timmins to North Bay was upgraded. The men lived in camps, and each camp had six gangs. They felled trees, cut branches, burned brush, drilled rock by hand, blew up stumps and rock, and one gang worked with the "poor man's banjo," the shovel. The new number 11 highway opened up that year, with two paved lanes. A new road meant a smoother trip to the south, but not much change for Temagami in any other way. It was still a modest little place where frame buildings stood side by side with log cabins, and where the provision of sidewalks was the responsibility of store owners. The most striking building was still the elegant fieldstone station.

Although the Second World War slowed post-Depression growth in the area, it does give us an indication of how much Temagami had grown since the Great War. In the 1914–18 war, 33 residents had joined up and 4 did not return. In the 1939–45 conflict, 100 men served their country and 8 were killed in active service.

In 1951 the Ontario Provincial Police received the first radio-equipped launch in the province to patrol Lake Temagami. That was also the year the exploits of a local pilot were featured in *Time* magazine. Lou Riopelle located a ski-equipped plane out of North Bay that had got stuck fast in spring slush on a northwestern Quebec

Waiting for the Buzz, *a small, fast launch of the 1920s.* OA 15380 102

Old-timers relaxing at Bear Island, date unknown.

lake. The downed pilot had spent a cold night in his plane's doorless cabin before Riopelle spotted him. Realizing what the problem was, Riopelle decided that he was not about to get caught in the same slushy trap, so he made a slow run across the surface of the lake, his ground speed slowed to 30 miles per hour and his skis barely skimming the ice. The North Bay pilot started to run and as the plane came alongside, he grabbed for a strut. Feeling the jolt as the extra weight hit his plane, Riopelle gave it full throttle. The other man swung his feet onto the right strut and half clambered and was half dragged inside. This completed the first on-the-fly, ground-to-air rescue that old-time bush pilots could recall.

In 1968 Temagami was incorporated as an Improvement District with a council appointed by the province. Ten years later the municipal representatives were elected and had responsibility for a much larger area.

From the 1960s to the present, Temagami's image has changed drastically. It is no longer seen as mainly a quiet tourist-oriented community, but is now a forum for widely differing political viewpoints. Consequently, the area has seen the rise of a number of ecology- and economy-oriented organizations over these years.

The Temagami Lakes Association, formed in 1931 by cottagers on the lake, by the 1970s saw its concerns as water quality, the preservation of the area at the expense of logging close to the lake, acid rain, and increased tourist traffic, which in its view lessened the enjoyment of lakeland life. A locally sponsored initiative, the Temagami Regional Studies Institute, was set up in 1978 to determine the environmental concerns of the area. A much more aggressive group, the Temagami Wilderness Society, was formed in 1986, primarily to protect the centuries-old pine trees from logging. Members of this organization were not only area property-owners but conservationists from across the continent with ties to other groups such as Greenpeace. By contrast, Northcare was organized to conserve the land as a viable economic entity.

Permanent residents and the Chamber of Commerce, too, are interested in promoting economic growth in the area. This stance came to prominence with the closure of the Sherman iron ore mine and the depletion of wood reserves for the Milne and other lumber companies.

The Temagami Indians have their own ideas of what's right for the area. In 1973 the band obtained a land caution. This effectively prevents new uses on the land. A major tourist development had been proposed at Maple Mountain, 48 kilometres to the north, and the Indians obtained the caution because they had never signed treaties with either the federal or the provincial government and they claimed much of the surrounding territory. As a result 10,360 square kilometres in 110 townships were closed to development.

The provincial government found itself unable to placate any of these interest groups even though money was given to the community to develop tourist potential and new parks were announced. An Advisory Council was formed to determine advantageous and ecologically sound land use and potential for the area. But in the fall of 1989 an extension of the Red Squirrel Road north of Temagami was built to access old-growth pine for further cutting, and the kettle came to the boil. Construction was blocked and hindered by the Wilderness Society, the Lakes Association, and the Indians, resulting in a provincial policing bill of over a million dollars.

There was no official cemetery in Temagami until 1983, and when one was established, it was appropriately named "Whispering Pines." The great trees have come to be a symbol of Temagami.   •

An almost forgotten grave marks an abandoned cemetery on Temagami Island.
Lynne Birnie

Teme-Augama Anishnabai

THE three main Indian tribes in northern Ontario are the Cree, Ojibwa, and Algonquin. The Timiskaming band is Algonquin, as are the Temagami, but they came under Ojibwa influence. Their dialect is from the Ojibwa, but few people speak it today.

The Iroquois raided the area from 1650 to 1700. Some bands, such as the Nipissing, suffered greatly, actually leaving their lands for a time, but the Temagamis were more fortunate; their homeland was away from the major canoe routes and encounters with the marauders tended to be mostly on the fringes of their territory.

Some events from that time have become entrenched in band lore. One legend tells how two small islands north of Garden Island received the same name — Stinking Island. One hot summer the Temagamis met their enemies the Iroquois in a mighty battle at this spot. Bodies from both tribes were left to rot in the sun, hence "Stinking Island." At Rabbit Lake, on the route to Lake Timiskaming, another legend tells us, a party of Iroquois raiders was camped on an island. Enterprising Temagamis sneaked onto the island in the night and slit the bottoms of the enemy's canoes. The next day the Iroquois were caught in the water in their sinking canoes and easily vanquished. The Temagamis, it appears, were not above using trickery to gain a victory. Once,

An Indian guide and his family. OA 13889-41

as Iroquois raiders paddled up the Temagami River, they saw a lynx swimming in the water and gave chase. In reality the "lynx" was no more than a skin, a decoy pulled by a Temagami warrior who led the Iroquois to a spot where they could be easily picked off from the land. Another legend tells of a single Temagami canoe caught by Iroquois some 60 kilometres north of Lake

Bear Island Hudson's Bay Company post, at the turn of the century.   Verla Pacey Collection

Temagami at the junction of the Lady Evelyn and Montreal rivers. After a desperate marathon paddle the Temagamis finally outdistanced their pursuers and alerted their people on Lake Temagami. That night, as the Iroquois slept on an island, a band of Temagamis set their foes' canoes adrift and later finished them off as they swam to the mainland.

Mute evidence of defensive positions used for lookouts and ambush sites during the struggles with the Iroquois may be found in pits, from 1.5 to 2.5 metres in diameter, which still survive, generally situated on high bluffs at Iroquois Point, Garden Island, Temagami Island, and several other locations.

An ancient Temagami myth centres on the North Arm of Lake Temagami. The people, it is said, sought more water for their parched land from Gitchie Manitou, the great spirit. He threw them water from the sea. The largest drops became Lake Temagami and the other nearby lakes. Enter a bad spirit, Matche Manitou. He came to live on Devil Island and plagued the people with blackflies before moving to Devil Mountain, opposite the island. A woman was given to Matche Manitou as a wife. The people respected her as *Kokomis* or grandmother, but she was not able to alter Matche Manitou's evil ways. After many quarrels with him she fled into the lake. But he threw four chunks of rock at her; these became islands. She came ashore on a fifth, larger than the rest, which is today called Granny

The sun rises on the North-East Arm of Lake Temagami.
Andy Stevens

Island. Matche Manitou, in a last gesture of hate before leaving the area, turned her to stone. Matche Manitou's handiwork remains — a small rock on the shore of Granny Island resembles a woman with her head between her hands.

Author Madeline Theriault is also known as Ka Kita Wa Pa No Kwe, the Wise Day Woman. In *Moose to Moccasins* she reflects on her people's ways. Life, she says, was hard but never dull. The forest provided most of what was needed for survival. The birch gave syrup and its bark could be made into cups and containers of various sizes. Folded and slipped into a long split stick, the bark made a long-lasting lantern. The trees gave the people material for snowshoes and *ti-ki-ma-gun*, or papoose boards for carrying babies. The babies were wrapped in rabbit-skin blankets; it took 90 skins to make one. Their diapers were made from moss cut in blocks and dried on tree stumps above the snow. They played with rattles made from duck bills strung together or inflated partridge craws filled with dried buds. Game from the forest and fish from the lakes and rivers were generally boiled, and fish broth was a nourishing hot drink. A special treat was hot cakes made by squashing fish eggs into flour and baking the result.

The old name for the Temagamis, Teme-Augama Anishnabai, or the Deep-Water People, has been brought back into common use in recent years. The tribe had six totems, or family emblems: the loon, the caribou, the rattlesnake, the porcupine, the kingfisher, and the beaver. A recent Chief, Gary Potts, is from the porcupine clan. The band has a flag which shows earth and sky centred with a white circle representing the seasons. A drum within the circle is the heartbeat of the motherland. Outside the circle, four feathers represent the compass points, and within it are the six clan emblems.

Madeline Theriault's brief autobiography shed light on native customs. She is seen here in 1930.
OA 9164 15139

At the centre, the sun represents the seed of life.

The Temagamis were a nomadic people who gathered each summer at Wabikon on Temagami Island. There was a communal system of law and later the chief was democratically elected. The Robinson-Huron Treaty of 1850 covered lands north and east of Lake Huron but it omitted any mention of the Temagamis. Although they received gifts and annuities over the years, they made no political link with any government. In 1884 a 259-square-kilometre reserve was surveyed at the south end of Lake Temagami, but this became the Temagami Forest Reserve. Although the federal government pressed the province to resolve the matter of the aboriginal people, land continued to be lost to flooding for hydro and to other provincial requirements. Gradually the Temagami band lost even customary hunting and fishing rights.

In the 1930s the Royal Canadian Legion supported the band in its attempts to gain a settlement, for many of the Temagamis were veterans. But not until 1943, when Canada purchased Bear Island from Ontario for $3,000, did the Temagamis have a home base, and then it was less than 283 hectares. From that time forward the band has attempted to regain its heritage via court action. In the band office an extensive library has been built up asserting their right to their land claims. In 1973 this library was useful when the band obtained the land caution preventing further exploitation of traditional Indian land while legal avenues were pursued.

The Teme-Augama Anishnabai have been struggling for more then a century and have spent huge sums of money to obtain their traditional lands and some compensation. To this date, they still have no settlement. •

Andy Stevens

Washaquonasin

Bill Guppy
Helen Hall

A Parks Canada poster of Grey Owl.

GREY Owl, the legendary author and conservationist, is buried near Waskesieu, Saskatchewan, in Prince Albert National Park, not far from the little cabin where he lived while studying beaver for the Canadian government. In the eight years before his death he wrote four books, classics of wilderness writing, in each of which he told only a little about his life and work. Since his death, this man has been the subject of several books and countless articles, yet gaps in his background still elude researchers. Grey Owl had good reason for not revealing the whole story of his life while he lived, and the contradictions in it have attracted public interest ever since his death.

This was a man famous as a champion of wildlife and nature, who for many years was a trapper. He claimed to be of Scots-Apache descent with experience in the American west: in fact he was reared by two maiden aunts and his grandmother in the English seaside town of Hastings. He relished the solitary life but managed romantic liaisons with five women.

Archibald Stansfeld Belaney was 17 when he came to Canada from Hastings. He made his way first to Timiskaming and the following year to Temagami. Bill Guppy, a noted woodsman, took a liking to the lanky youngster when he saw him at the Temagami train station. The boy was broke and had nowhere to stay,

so Bill took him in and fed him. Guppy's stories satisfied Archie's keen interest in the life of a trapper, and the lad became somewhat of an apprentice in woodland lore. Archie seemed able to handle animals

with ease, and, of equal importance in that isolated settlement, he was an accomplished pianist; his playing enlivened numerous dances and parties. Later, Archie took seasonal work as a guide and forest ranger, and gradually the tenderfoot changed and became an accepted woodsman. He was observant and careful in the bush, but he seemed to crave attention. He kept a razor-sharp axe that he threw at marks on trees and walls. His accuracy never failed to impress onlookers — splitting a $2 bill with an axe at a distance was no mean feat.

Archie became a guide for the Temagami Inn and delivered mail by dog team in winter. This led him to meet Angele Eguana, a member of the Nebenegwane family of the Temagami Indian band. Angele had no formal education, but she was well-schooled in her people's ways and comfortable in the forest. She could speak only Ojibwa in 1907 when she went to work at the Temagami Inn. She was 19, the same age as Archie. By now Archie was tanned, fit, and handsome, with his long hair tied back in a ponytail and a desperate hunger to become more involved with the Indians. It was inevitable that he and the pretty native girl would get together.

In later years Archie was to say that his time at Temagami gave him most of his bush knowledge. He wintered at Bear Island and began to live the Indian life he had dreamed about. He felt peace in the forest and kinship with the native people. They in turn sensed his commitment and shared with him their beliefs as well as their customs. They gave him the nickname "Owl" for his intense concentration; he added the "Grey" later. Since he liked to travel at night, his new friends also called him *Washaquonasin*, which means "he who walks by night."

Archie and Angele were married at Bear Island in 1910. They lived for one winter in a tent, where their daughter, Agnes, was born. Watching one day as Angele used a powder made from a rotted poplar tree to sooth a rash on the baby's thighs, Archie realized

A portrait of Grey Owl and his publisher Lovat Dickson taken about 1935.

that it darkened the skin. He began to rub himself with this powder daily; it was one more step toward becoming an Indian.

His knowledge of Ojibwa was improving, and he was accepted by the band, but Archie was restless by nature. In 1912 he left his family to travel. Angele was upset but she accepted his decision. Archie had the notion that Indians were free, not tied to one locale. He did not fail to notice that the Indian homeland was becoming a white man's playground, and this fact gave a bitter edge to his romantic dreams.

The man who would be an Indian headed west to another wilderness area. Biscotasing is situated half-way between Sudbury and Chapleau on the CPR line.

At "Bisco" he became a riverman and a fire ranger. I lived at Bisco for a while in the 1950s and I met people there who recalled Archie Belaney. His landlady, Mrs. Legace, told how her boarder used to sit in front of the mirror night after night, running the bowl of a spoon over his nose. Gradually he bent the cartilage, giving himself a classic profile. Now, except for his blue eyes, he had in every respect the appearance of a native. He began to embroider his story and to weave an Indian childhood into accounts of his early life. He left Bisco in 1914 to spend some time in Nova Scotia with the Micmacs, leaving behind him a Métis girl, Marie Girard, pregnant with his child.

During the Great War Archie swapped his buckskins

for the garb of a sniper on the western front. On leave, he visited England. In Hastings, the two aunts who had raised him after he was deserted by his mother were delighted to see him. He made no mention to them of his masquerade as an Indian. Why should he? Back in Canada he certainly never mentioned Hastings. They took him in later, after he was wounded and sent home to recuperate. During his convalescence, he met a childhood friend, Constance Holmes, and married her. After he was invalided out of the army with a small disability pension, however, Constance made it clear that Canada held no appeal for her, and, true to form, Archie left his bride behind when he sailed.

He returned to Biscotasing and lived there until 1925, periodically returning to Temagami to work. These absences may have something to do with the fact that the returned soldier had taken up his old axe- and knife-throwing ways, often to the alarm of those nearby.

In addition, he had begun to drink heavily and was becoming a notorious fighter. He had to leave Bisco from time to time to avoid assault charges. Nonetheless, Grey Owl had considerable charm and, now in his early thirties, stood out as a tall, bronzed, handsome figure with a thin hawk-like face and long braids. Angele, always captivated by her wandering husband, conceived a son during a 1922 visit from him.

In 1925 Grey Owl took a guiding job at Camp Wabikon on Lake Temagami. He became reacquainted with his daughter, Agnes, now 13, and one night, he squired her to a dance. There he met Gertie Bernard, an Iroquois from Mattawa who was working at the camp for the summer. He was much taken with her evident poise, education and intelligence. Naturally, the relationship intensified; he began to call her by the Indian name *Anahareo*. When winter came Anahareo returned to Mattawa and Grey Owl returned to Angele for a while,

Anahareo played a large part in Grey Owl's metamorphosis from trapper to conservationist.

Grey Owl feeds a beaver kit with a bottle.

but old habits reasserted themselves and in 1926 he left Temagami, never to return. He found another wilderness, this time in Quebec, near Abitibi, and soon Anahareo joined him there. He had been fluent in Ojibwa for many years, and she had no idea he was not an Indian.

The beaver and other fur-bearers in that area had become scarce due to over-trapping and it was hard to make a living. Anahareo encouraged in Grey Owl an interest in preserving nature rather than living at the expense of it. He began to write about the wilderness and found a ready market in newspapers and magazines. The change was a gradual one, but as Grey Owl saw how the land and wildlife had been abused by over-harvesting, he stopped trapping and became an advocate for the wilderness. From 1928 to 1931 he and Anahareo lived in the bush at Cabano, Témiscoutia, south of the St. Lawrence, and Grey Owl began the work which would fill the rest of his life — fighting for conservation in general and an understanding of the beaver in particular.

He kept two orphaned beaver kits in his cabin, later building a special house onto it for them to live in, and he studied them, making short films about them and about life in the wilderness. By now the Canadian government had begun to take notice of his work and his writing. He was appointed first to Riding Mountain National Park in Manitoba and then to Prince Albert National Park in Saskatchewan to look after beaver conservation programs. This was the most productive period of his life. Between 1931 and 1936 he wrote three adult books and one for children. *Men of the Last Frontier* (1931), *Pilgrims of the Wild* (1934), *The Adventures of Sajo and Her Beaver People* (1935), and *Tales of an Empty Cabin* (1936) were all international best-sellers.

Lovat Dickson, Grey Owl's publisher at Macmillan of Canada, arranged lecture tours in Great Britain, where he was especially popular. His audiences were fascinated as he demonstrated with stories, sketches, and his films how the beaver lived. He certainly must have been a riveting sight to the English, dressed as he was in beaded moosehide and fringes and fixing his audience with a piercing gaze. During his second British lecture tour he had a command performance at Buckingham Palace. The Royal Family was spellbound by his talk, and the Princess Elizabeth begged him not to stop but to tell more of the wild.

Between lecture tours Grey Owl maintained and developed his Indian biography. The magazine *Canadian*

Forest and Outdoors reprinted the text of a speech he gave to the Canadian Forestry Association with a lengthy introduction in which they used verbatim the background he had provided, right down to this early life as a part-Apache. He came to be seen as a modern-day Hiawatha. In spite of the deception, Grey Owl's evident sincerity about his subject captured the hearts of millions. When he wrote, "The wilderness should no longer be considered a playground for vandals, or a rich treasure trove to be ruthlessly exploited for personal gain...," they were moved. As they believed in him when he said, "I laid aside my rifle and traps and like Paul, worked for the betterment of those whom I had so assiduously persecuted."

His frequent extended absences strained his relationship with Anahareo, who was much more independent than Angele. Grey Owl was so busy he hardly noticed, but in 1936 Anahareo left him for good. The parting was amicable, but interestingly, Anahareo remarked at the time that if she ever wrote about their time together, the book's title would be *Devil in Deerskins*. Many years later she did write that book and that indeed was the title.

As for Grey Owl, he soon met up with a Métis woman named Yvonne Perrier and married her — for a while.

In early 1938 Grey Owl returned to Canada after his second British tour. He appeared at Toronto's Massey Hall in March of that year, but within a month he was dead. He died at his home in Prince Albert National Park. Sheer exhaustion brought on by stress and a demanding schedule coupled with a bout of pneumonia killed the wilderness man at the age of 50.

But Grey Owl's untimely death did not end his story. Some years earlier a young *North Bay Nugget* reporter, Britt Jessup, had heard rumours about Grey Owl's past. He had travelled to Temagami to interview Angele. She was still captivated by her errant husband's memory but saw no reason not to admit that he was a white man. Incredibly — by today's standards anyway — Jessup and his editor had sat on the story for three years. They reasoned that the man was doing a great job for Canadian conservation and that his message would be harmed if the truth came out. Both felt freed from their self-imposed silence by Grey Owl's death. The *Nugget* broke a world newspaper scoop and the North American Indian Grey Owl was exposed as Archie Belaney, Englishman.

People could not believe the great deception. Even Lovat Dickson, his publisher, had been certain that Grey Owl was an Indian. A media debate raged for some considerable time over whether the *Nugget*'s story was correct. Grey Owl was a hoaxer and a rogue, but, with time, the public came to realize the benefits he had brought to his adopted country. The wanderer who could be tied neither to family nor to a narrow interpretation of the truth had been the North's greatest publicist. He had drawn attention to inhumane trapping and to the waste of precious natural resources. Just before he died, Grey Owl wrote, "The forest is not inexhaustible as many think it is and like several species of game concerning which the public cherish the same delusion, it will come to a quick end."

Grey Owl's message rings true today. He said, "Any interference with nature is damnable. Not only nature but the people will suffer. I want to arouse in Canadian people a sense of their responsibility, the great responsibility they have for that north country and its inhabitants, human and animal." The wilderness man would not be silent were he alive in Temagami today. He would be a leader in the fight for the forest and an advocate for the Indian band. The Grey Owl Festival held in the place where he learned his craft would cheer him. The commemorative plaque in Finlayson Park would give him pleasure, as would the knowledge that a lake bears his name. Grey Owl's books have delighted an international following for almost 60 years, and though their author had his faults he will long be seen as a man who created an image of northern Canada which has stood the test of time.   •

Some Characters

FRONTIERS have always attracted eccentrics, striking personalities, and just plain different people. Northern Ontario was no exception and Temagami had its share. There was Big George Friday, for instance, said to be the strongest man in the area at the turn of the century. Six-foot, 250-pound Friday carried huge amounts of freight from the Temagami Inn dock to its warehouse. And, by contrast, there was Temagami Ned, a short, skinny chap who carried an alarm clock strung around his neck, and who popped up from time to time to amuse tourists, offering to pose for photographs in exchange for a big cigar.

Grey Owl apart, three men stand out in any list of those whose lives touched Temagami. All three might well have said that they failed in significant aspects of their lives. The reader can be the judge, but at least these men deserve to be remembered.

THE BUSINESS PIONEER

DAN O'Connor was born in Pembroke in 1864. He dabbled in prospecting and lumbering in Mattawa before moving on to Sudbury, where he switched to the hotel business. He became the town's mayor at only 30. Security held no appeal, however, and between 1894 and 1897 O'Connor ventured out on prospecting

Temagami Ned with members of his band. OA 6496 S11288
His alarm clock is nowhere to be seen.

trips, canoeing into Temagami country and staking the Iron Lake, Vermilion Lake, and Ko-Ko-Ko properties. O'Connor had the vision to determine the future tourist potential of Lake Temagami as well as its mining prospects, and when he found that the Ontario Northland line would pass well east of the lake, he was alarmed. He personally lobbied Queen's Park for a change of direction, even going so far as to bring several Members

Sometime around 1910, a confident Dan O'Connor at right, stood for his picture to be taken beside his Belle of Temagami.

OA 9348 S14644

of Parliament up to see the area for themselves.

He was successful, but the hustling entrepreneur did not wait for the rails to provide transportation. He picked up a small steamer, the *Marie*, in the Mattawa area and sailed it up Lake Timiskaming, where he proceeded to use horse teams and hard labour to haul it up snow- and ice-bound rivers in sections to Lake Temagami. Investors are always ready to join up with a mover like Dan O'Connor, and he formed a syndicate to help him see his plans come to fruition. He established the Temagami Boat Line and had a hotel, the Halfway

House, built before the railway arrived, and his syndicate spent $20,000, then a large sum, to build the Temagami Inn on Temagami Island. The Lady Evelyn Hotel came next, and when his flagship, the *Belle of Temagami*, was finished, he could reflect on a promising future.

Dan O'Connor was popular; he mixed well with people and he was often referred to as the "King" — or at least the "Lord" — of Temagami. Grey Owl once recalled a visit to the lake by a railway magnate who wanted to go duck hunting. Midsummer is not the right time for this sport, but O'Connor was not fazed — he had some ducks shipped in on the train. Next day, out on the lake, an Indian friend released the ducks from the cover of an island, the sportsman blazed away, and the spoils were brought to him strung on a pole. The worthy hunter never even noticed that his ducks were of the barnyard variety.

When, in rapid succession, the Lady Evelyn Hotel burned down and the Temagami Inn was damaged by fire, his mining claims were not picked up, and the Boat Line faced stiff competition on the lake, O'Connor decided that his luck was strained at Temagami and it was time to make some new luck elsewhere. He moved north to Connaught, just in time for the Porcupine gold rush. Ever a hustler, he built a general store and a sawmill, and continued to prospect up until his death in 1933.

Dan O'Connor packed several careers into his lifetime. He made money in Temagami, but always felt that he had failed to really reach the business potential of the lake. But consider his legacy: he secured a new route for the railway and began the hospitality and transportation industry; one mine, the Big Dan, bore his name, and claims he staked and sold to Sir William Mulock and others became the great Sherman Mine 70 years later. He never knew that his feat of bringing the steamer overland would one day be noted by Ripley's *Believe It or Not*. Perhaps that would have pleased Dan O'Connor most of all.

THE CREATIVE IMPOSTER

JUST prior to the Depression, a critically acclaimed silent movie was made in the Temagami area. Grey Owl had left the lake for good by this time, but he would have found common ground with one of the two principal actors. Both had "changed" their race, Archie Belaney rejecting his white background to become an Indian and the man we can call Sylvester rejecting his black heritage for the same end.

Sylvester Long was born in 1890 and grew up in the northern states. He may actually have been part Indian, for his skin was not very dark. He picked up a few words of Cherokee working for a circus and decided early that an Indian would have more chance of being accepted by white society than would a black man. He was a handsome man with great athletic ability — he ran with Jim Thorpe and once had sparred rounds with Jack Dempsey. Sylvester faked his birth certificate, absorbed all he could about Indian culture, and adopted the persona of Long Lance of the Cherokee tribe. He was able to attend an Indian residential school and almost managed to get into West Point. He served in the ranks in the First World War, although he later indicated that he had been an officer. Unfortunately, his biography and background changed and expanded to suit the circumstances, and whenever his ancestry was questioned, Sylvester was forced to move on.

Unlike Grey Owl, Sylvester wore ordinary street clothes except when he was among Indian people. He used his "Indian" background and a talent for writing to become a reporter, working on papers across western Canada, and his stories about Indians were popular. After he spent some time with a tribe in Alberta, he added the name "Buffalo Child" to Long Lance.

On vacations he stayed with the Blackfoot in the

The Belle of Temagami *leaves the town for its daily run sometime in 1942.*

Verla Pacey

United States, studying them and finally writing a book about their customs. He wrote a number of popular articles on the Custer massacre, taking such obvious liberties with the facts that the U.S. Commissioner of Indian Affairs declared them to be works of fiction.

Buffalo Child Long Lance had a long run of luck, and eventually his handsome looks and fine physique came to the attention of Hollywood. He was offered the lead in a silent movie, the story of Indians struggling to survive the harsh land and their salvation when a herd of caribou finally appears. The film was called *The Silent Enemy*, and it was made around Rabbit Chutes, just east of Temagami. It was possibly one of the most authentic native epics ever. It was shot in fall and winter using sets and equipment all made by area natives. Angele Belaney and a host of others found employment that winter making clothes and a variety of props. When shooting finished, Long Lance abruptly left Temagami and returned to New York, perhaps alarmed that Angele had mentioned that he was rather dark to be an Indian, and that his native co-star had remarked on his punctuality, not a common Indian trait.

He kept up his image as a public figure, was accepted into the prestigious Explorers' Club, and wrote another book, this time on Indian sign language. But the façade cracked when a lawyer retained by the moviemakers checked his background and confronted him. The fitness enthusiast turned to drink and hired out as a bodyguard to a California socialite. The strain of covering his tracks and the decline in his physical prowess became too much to bear, and in 1932 Sylvester shot himself.

Sylvester, alias Buffalo Child Long Lance, genuinely loved Indian people and Indian life, but he wanted to live in two worlds. He could not accept one completely, as did Grey Owl. His will left his savings to schools and to the Alberta reserve he had visited. After Grey Owl died, the public seized on his story, but Long Lance simply faded from the news. Except for rare prints of *The Silent Enemy*, there is no evidence left of his few months in Temagami.

THE REBEL OBLATE

A historical plaque at Verner, between Sudbury and North Bay, states that Charles Paradis was responsible for bringing settlers to the area at the turn of the century. The plaque tells nothing about Charles Paradis really, nothing about his dreams, his battles, or the controversial figure he cut. His name is perpetuated by a bay on Lake Timiskaming, but there is little else to recall him. This is too bad, for the short, stocky, black-

Father Paradis

The church on Bear Island.
Andy Stevens

Father Paradis and friends.

robed Oblate priest was famous in the North in his time.

Father Paradis was born in Kamouraska, Quebec, in 1848, and became a priest in his thirties. He was captivated by Lake Temagami on his first visit, and conceived the idea of colonizing the area with French-Canadian farmers. This aim he single-mindedly pursued for the rest of his life. For him, Temagami was a veritable Garden of Eden. Unfortunately, the church did not share his view. For several years he quarrelled with his superiors over his campaign to prevent over-logging on the Ottawa River, and over a scheme to flood that river valley to aid navigation. To discipline him, they sent him to a house of his order in Buffalo in 1888, but nothing could silence him, and eventually he was physically ejected from the residence and expelled from the order. Paradis didn't even pause: he still called himself an Oblate, wooed the press, wrote complimentary articles about the land between Sturgeon Falls and Temagami, and secured a contract from Ontario to bring 2,000 settlers to Vernor and Sturgeon Falls at a fee of $3 a head.

An emissary of the bishop responsible for northeastern Ontario reported after meeting Paradis that he was "dangerous, disturbed...his schemes a fraud." It is a wonder he actually managed to get to see the good father at all. Paradis canoed with some followers to James Bay, did some prospecting on the return, and still had time to check out the place presently known as Ville Marie, Quebec, for possible settlement. He also invented *Le Maringoinfuge*, a foul-smelling but effective fly dope made from Stockholm tar, citronella, and lard. With another bishop's endorsement on the label the stuff sold well.

Paradis chose Sandy Inlet at the far north of Lake Temagami to be the capital of what he said in 1895 would be "a province within a province." Two missionaries and more than a dozen followers helped him clear 40.5 hectares of bush. Cabins, a chapel, a blacksmith's shop, a fruit cellar, and an icehouse were built there. The aim was for the settlement to be self-sufficient. On a hillside, a large cross towered over the mission Paradis called Sacre Coeur.

When angry church officials succeeded in having his colonization grants cut off in 1897, the busy father prospected and even worked in a mine for a while to raise funds. From 1897 to just before his death, his settlement became a home for orphaned French-

Canadian boys. They received schooling, tended to farm chores, and sold produce to Keewaydin and other camps and resorts. Paradis paddled 27 kilometres each Sunday to take mass on Bear Island.

In 1911 he set up a halfway house for men en route from the rail line to the Porcupine gold fields. Not content simply to accept their money for the privilege of sleeping on the soft side of board cots, he caught the gold bug from them and headed north, where he blew up a worthless vein on the edge of Night Hawk Lake. The vein may have had no value, but the explosion had the effect of pulling the plug on the lake; the major waterway to the new gold mines was reduced to a soggy muskeg. Paradis tried to say he had found alluvial soil for farming, but a vengeful province and angry miners forced to carry their canoes convinced him to flee to Michigan for a while.

Paradis was a man of many interests. He collected Italian art, painted watercolours which were a fine representation of Timiskaming life, and compiled an Ojibwa-French dictionary. Tragically, in 1924 a fire consumed much of this work and destroyed the settlement buildings. Paradis and his followers were forced to leave Temagami, and he died in Montreal two years later.

Charles Paradis was a mix of dreamer and builder. His grand design failed, but Vernor, Sturgeon Falls, and Ville Marie remain. All that is left of the mission of Sacre Coeur, now the site of Camp Wanapitei, is the icehouse. Paradis would have been happy with Camp Wanapitei. The main chateau and the log bridge over the river were beautifully crafted by Finnish carpenters, and the camp's large garden makes it almost self-sufficient. Some relics of his dream are preserved at the camp, including a fragment of the cross he boldly raised above his colony in the wilderness.   •

Andy Stevens

Boats

The docks were often jammed with boats in the early 1930s.   Verla Pacey

LAKE Temagami has been used for both transport and pleasure ever since the first aboriginal people ventured onto it in their dugouts. Canoes are still a common sight as cottagers and trippers ply their way through the inlets and around the islands of the great lake, but Temagami also saw a heyday of steam.

Steamers arrived at Temagami before the railway did. Commercial vessels appeared on Lake Temiskaming as early as 1882, having come by way of the Ottawa River, but there was no easy route for the large boats to get to Lake Temagami. A local entrepreneur, Dan O'Connor, eventually obtained a small steamer, the *Marie*, and packed it in over the winter ice to establish the Temagami Boat Line. The arrival of the Temiskaming & Northern Ontario Railway brought the *Beaver Queen* and the *Wanda*. They came in by flat car and were added to the roster of the Boat Line, which now had regular connections to Bear Island, the Temagami Inn, and the Lady Evelyn Hotel to the north.

Competition to the Boat Line came in the form of the Temagami Navigation Company with its boats, the *Bobs* and the *Temagami*, a long, narrow former pleasure yacht purchased from the Eaton family in Muskoka. Later the *Keego* was added to the fleet. The Boat Line countered with the addition of the *Spry*, and in 1908 they launched the biggest boat ever to operate on the lake. Built

locally, the *Belle of Temagami* was at that time the largest vessel north of Manitoulin Island. She was 108 feet long with a 24-foot beam and one funnel. Her three decks carried up to 300 passengers.

Most boats were laid up for the duration of the First World War, and camps on the lake suffered from a lack of dependable transport. Toward the end of the war, boats began to be converted from steam to gasoline; the *Keego* was the first conversion. The Boat Line

The Bobs *at Cochrane's Camp, 1931*

if the boat was on time it arrived at the village again by 6:15 P.M. Fares ranged from a return of $3 to Wabikon to $4.25 to Keewaydin. Rarely did the boat stop any longer than the time needed to drop passengers and freight and make a pick-up.

Dennis Houghton's family built a cottage in the 1930s on Island 86. Before the construction of the lake access road in the 1970s all traffic passed by their cottage en route from Temagami to the Hub of the lake. Today that stretch of lake is much quieter. Dennis recalls the heyday of the long-nosed wooden launches typical of Temagami in the 1930s. Generally 30 feet long, most had small cabins towards the rear. Though they were graceful in the water, they could be as skittish in a

An Associated Press group boarding the Belle of Temagami *in 1913.*

was sold in 1918, and the new owners added service to Keewaydin Camp and Camp Wanapitei. They also added a new vessel, the *Kokomis*. This boat was glassed in for much of her length and boasted curtains for passenger privacy. The fast mahogany-strip boat would be the longest-serving craft on the lake. In 1924 the Boat Line changed hands again, this time going to Captain Ted Guppy, who brought in a handsome new vessel, the *Iona*, from the Lake of Bays. The line operated until 1936, when it gave way to Captain John Sproat's Temagami Boat Company.

The 1929 timetable for the *Belle of Temagami* offers an insight into the service available for residents and tourists of the time. The boat left Temagami docks at 10:15 A.M. and proceeded to the Hub and Camp Wabikon. Passengers headed south to Camp Accouchiching, transferred to another boat from Wabikon, while the *Belle* went on to Friday's Point (where it had to be flagged), the Temagami Inn, Bear Island, Garden Island, another flag stop, and finally to Keewaydin Camp, arriving there at 2:30 P.M. The reserve order was taken on the return, and

The staff of Boatlines Restaurant in 1949. J. R. Stevens/MacLean Photo

Jack Swann, who was the manager of the company in the 1950s and 1960s, before the demand for its services dwindled, recalled some of the boats used then. The barges *Cross Lake* and *Sharp Rock* ferried bulk items, and three slick former air-sea rescue launches, the *Wakemika*, *Gull Lake*, and *Sesikinika*, had a variety of uses for express and charter. Most business travellers opted for the *Wendigo*, the fastest boat on the lake at the time. The OPP took over policing the lake in 1949, and their light and dark blue launch, the *Temagami*, was said to have a top speed of 40 knots. It was a 22-foot boat built by Shepherd's of Niagara-on-the-Lake and was powered by 115-horsepower Chrysler engines.

Three boats offered passenger service until the mid-1960s. The *Naiad* operated on the South-West Arm, the *Vedette* ran to the South Arm, and the *Aubrey Cousins V.C.* plied the North Arm. Each day during the summer,

frothy chop, as are today's fibreglass-hulled boats. The water would hit the boat with a smacking noise, sending bow waves high before the wind and back to spray riders with what felt like volleys of broken glass.

The tourist and transport business slowed down on Lake Temagami during the Second World War, and John Sproat sold the boats still in operation to the railway in 1944. The Temiscaming & Northern Ontario Railway became the Ontario Northland Railway in 1946 and kept on running the Boat Company for another 20 years. New docks, offices, and waiting rooms were built, and the railway went beyond simple transportation to sell complete vacation trips with lodging, meals, etc. included.

Alas, the company lost its flagship in 1944. As the *Belle of Temagami* was being pulled out of the water for winter storage, the fir-and-poplar-crib beneath the structure collapsed with her weight, and the *Belle* broke her back. A broken keel finished 36 years of service on the lake.

Andy Stevens

Bill Crofut in his 1923 Hackercraft replica on Lake Temagami.

the whistles of these three were a welcome sound across the lake as they brought supplies and ferried vacationers.

The *Naiad* was a pretty boat. Built for Senator W. A. Sanford in 1893, she had been modelled after the royal yacht *Britannia*. The frame was a steel keel and ribs. The captain and steersman stood in an open area near the bow, and behind them the roof supports were angled slightly inward and the windows slanted. This, plus a 12-foot bowsprit, gave the boat's appearance an illusion of greater speed. The closed cabin, curtained for privacy, contained bird's-eye maple and black cherry panelling. The gold scrollwork on the bow and her sleek black-painted body made the *Naiad* one of the most elegant vessels on the lake.

Demand for the service had faded by 1965. The grand resorts were declining; several had closed or gone into private ownership. Shell Oil purchased the Boat Company from the railway and ran it for only a year before closing it down. All that remains today is a water-taxi service. Three boats were all that was left when the line ceased operations, and these were beached. The *Aubrey Cousins* was sold but later burned, and a federal inspector who examined the other two found some rotted planks on the *Naiad* and ordered both boats destroyed, even though they were still basically sound.

A red canoe reflects the peace of Temagami.
Andy Stevens

Although commercial water passenger transport has largely gone, the growth in private vessels has been rapid. There are boats of all sizes on the lake, from the popular steel-hulled work boats to open outboards, cabin cruisers, and even houseboats, yet Lake Temagami is so big that it never seems crowded. Boaters can still enjoy the lonely stillness of early morning, red and gold upon the water as the sun rises and the haunting cry of the loon echoes across the lake.

But not all boats on the lake are steel and aluminum. The canoe is still common, and here and there people preserve old ways with wooden boats. Some, like Peter Birnie of Island 585, restore old runabouts, and Bill Crofut of Island 356 at the former Northwoods Camp in the South-West Arm, harking back to his childhood enjoyment of the steamers, now builds his own. He has a 20-foot fantail canopy launch with a practically silent power of 5 knots using an electric motor. It has a white hull, a polished wooden deck, and an elegant fringed canopy, and Bill feels that it has the nicest ride of anything on the lake other than a canoe. His runabout, *Susie*, is a copy of a 1923 Hackercraft. The frame was built by Morgan Marine of Lake George, New York, and the snub-nosed, square-sterned boat has a driver's compartment, one behind for passengers, and a third to house the motor. Boats like Bill's *Susie* are a gracious link with Lake Temagami's past.   •

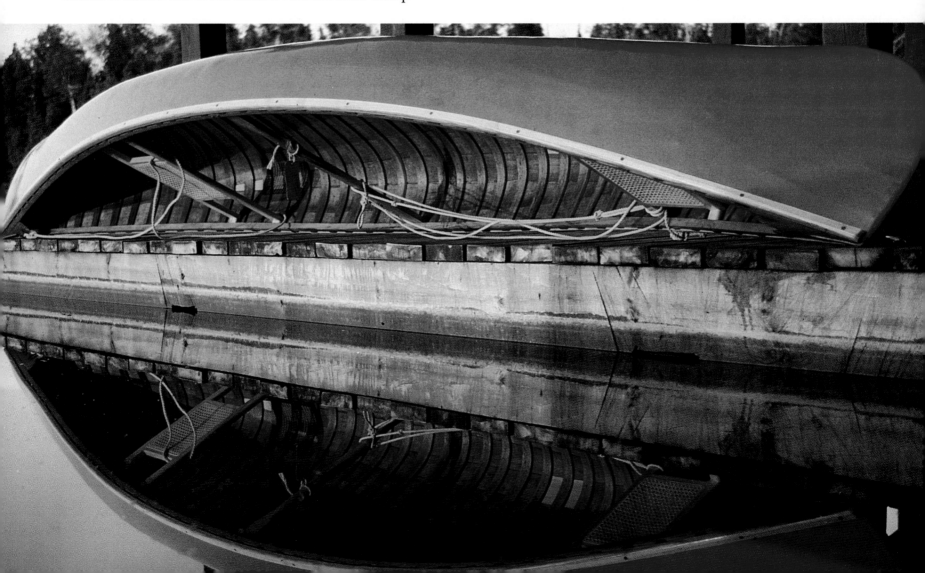

Cottages, Camps, and Hospitality

IN 1904 the province of Ontario sent a land surveyor to Temagami in answer to a challenge that had come the year before when canoeists from Cleveland had actually tried to claim land on the lake by occupation. The surveyor's report recommended that islands of 2 hectares or greater should be leased in two or more parcels. Frank Cochrane was Minister for Crown Lands at the time, and being well aware of the considerable sum that vacationers might spend in the area, he authorized 21-year cottage leases with an option to renew.

Cottages are by law restricted to the many numbered islands of Lake Temagami, and this has surely been one of the wiser recreational moves of the Ontario government. Island property requires water transport and boat maintenance and storage, and this has reduced casual usage of the lake somewhat, limiting most visitors to the camps and resorts. In addition, it restricts any accidental residential fires to a smaller area. In 1935 pressure from cottage owners brought about the declaration of a "skyline reserve" for Lake Temagami. This prohibited logging within 90 metres of the water in order to preserve the beauty of the pine-dominated skyline.

In many cases, the cottage leaseholds on the numbered islands have belonged to the same families for generations. The Funnell family, for instance, have leased Island 1,087 since 1922. Ken Wismer, a friend of the

The start of a canoe trip at Keewaydin. Keewaydin Camps

Funnells, was so captivated by the wilderness when he came to visit that he immediately applied for and received the lease on Island 1,086. Decades later, the next generation of Funnells and Wismers still celebrate annually their first campfire dinner on the lake. The menu offers now, as it did then, "chilled northern air with anticipation sauce" as an appetizer, pan-fried fillets of pickerel with boiled potatoes, and biscuits baked in a reflector oven, followed by clear black tea,

Old canoes hang from the dining-hall ceiling at Camp Wanapitei.
Lynne Birnie

prunes, and Horlicks malted milk tablets.

In addition to the hundreds of cottages, there are, of course, the camps and the resorts — 25 in the Lake Temagami region alone, many more if you count those in the Marten River and Field River Valley tourist areas to the south, and those in Latchford, Cobalt, and Elk Lake to the north.

The first place to stay in the village of Temagami was the Halfway House, a log building put up in 1895 by Dan O'Connor, the Temagami Boat Line's founder. The Temagami Hotel and Steamboat Company built the Ronnoco Hotel in 1905, and that was it until the Goddard Hotel came into being in 1934. The Ronnoco's name was later changed to the Minawassi, and before it burned down in 1973 it was making more money from the beverage room than from paying guests.

Early in the century there were three places to stay on the lake itself. The Hudson's Bay Company factor's wife, who was called Granny Turner by everyone, ran the Lakeview House on the southern tip of Bear Island; the Steamboat Company built the log Temagami Inn on Temagami Island in 1905; and soon after that the Lady Evelyn Hotel was built at an isolated location toward the north end of the lake. The Lady Evelyn, during its short existence, was a luxury resort despite its remoteness, and even played host to aristocracy — the Duke and Duchess of Connaught stayed there. Alas, the Lady Evelyn burned down in 1914 and was never rebuilt.

The Temagami Inn operated until 1943, when it became a private co-operative. The main lodge was a two-storey log building with 45 bedrooms. For those who wished more privacy, cabins set in the pines offered

The Ronnoco Hotel was named after Dan O'Connor;   J. R. Stevens
Ronnoco is O'Connor spelled backwards.

"sleep as a benediction." All bathrooms had hot and cold running water, and there was a large dining room and lounge. Separate buildings housed a clubhouse and a recreation pavilion where ballroom dancing was a popular evening activity. The Temagami Inn catered to families and provided fishing and shore lunches from its launch, the *Minnekahda*. A brochure from the late 1920s assures patrons that the clientele of the Inn will be strictly gentile. It also refers to the 104.5-kilometre drive from North Bay to Temagami as "thrilling." No doubt it means "bone-shaking," for that road was in bad shape for years. On arrival, cars were garaged in Temagami and passengers took the *Belle of Temagami* to the Inn.

When we talk about camps in Temagami it is important to differentiate: there are hunting and fishing camps, family camps, children's camps, and an occasional camp that might almost qualify as a luxury resort. Camp White Bear was one of these.

Located on Island 488 on the South-West Arm of

the lake, White Bear entertained celebrity guests in its heyday. It had been built by Edward Judson, a shrewd businessman who had given up his regular vocation to become the business manager — and first husband — of Rita Hayworth, and the guest list, by invitation only, included stars or those being groomed for stardom. Contracts were signed there, and some high-priced talent used the solitude — it was 46 watery kilometres to Temagami — to "dry out" from their alcohol problems. Guests were pampered with lighted pathways and baths in the guest cabins (it was the only lake property boasting that particular luxury). Shoes left outside the doors were polished overnight and breakfast could be delivered to cabins. Breakfast, like all other meals, was cooked by a top-flight chef, and all food was brought in fresh, no canned goods here. Guests — Cary Grant, Carole Lombard, James Stewart, and Bob Hope among them —

The Temagami Inn in its heyday.   J.C. Elliot, TLA

could relax in the pleasant 25.5-metre-long lodge, soaring high above the water's edge, while they listened to orchestra leader Percy Faith play the grand piano.

Fire destroyed the lodge in 1952, and debris from the building, including a large safe, tumbled into the deep, clear water. The strongbox (emptied of valuables) is still visible. Judson sold the property and it became a children's camp until 1976, when it was bought by private interests.

Not nearly as luxurious was Camp Accouchiching, located on Island 938. It opened in 1937, and Grey Owl's first wife, Angele, worked there along with their two children. A former guide, Alf Cook, explained that guides at Accouchiching really earned their wages. Fishing trips usually had two guests and one guide to each 18-foot close-ribbed Peterborough canoe. On

The Camp Eucaroma dining room showing the fireplace and rustic look of the 1920s.   A. M. Drenth

hot days it could be difficult to convince people that the evenings become very cool, and often guides had to be real diplomats to make sure that enough suitable clothing and equipment were carried by guests. Visitors were not usually handy in a canoe, so it was up to the guides to do most of the paddling — up to 32 kilometres a day — as well as the portaging. By the time they returned after a long day on the water, the passengers might be practically asleep. It was up to the guide to keep paddling, get them home, and clean any fish they had caught on return. Big fish were a boon; they often meant a more sizeable tip.

Grey Owl once observed that in the earlier years guides and tourists behaved as comrades on the trail; later the guide's role became more that of a servant. However, this probably depended on the type of camp. Wilderness camps fostered camaraderie, but at the resorts people paid to relax and be waited upon. Most of the children's camps promoted a wilderness experience.

Keewaydin, the oldest continually operating youth camp in North America, was established on Devil Island in the North Arm of Lake Temagami in 1901. Until the

Trippers paddling away from base camp at Camp Keewaydin.   Keewaydin Camps

The interior of the dining hall at Camp Keewaydin awaiting the arrival of campers.
Lynne Birnie

railway came to Temagami, campers made a six-day canoe trip from Mattawa to reach the base camp.

Keewaydin, which means "northwest wind" in Ojibwa, advertised solely in the United States. Early brochures assured that this was not a "make believe camp on a crowded lake," but rather a wilderness canoe experience to foster physical and moral growth. A camp newsletter, *The Kicker*, excited readers with talk of forest fires, wildlife, exploration of "new" lakes, and visits to Hudson's Bay Company forts. The camp's founder, Gregg Clarke, stressed endurance and character-building, an emphasis which was retained even through changes of ownership.

"To know a man's character you must camp with him" is the dictum followed by Keewaydin's young campers, and the "Keewaydin Way" is summed up in the motto, "I do not fear tomorrow, for today I am victorious, over the river, over the trail, and most of all, myself." The emphasis is heavily on canoe-tripping; time spent at the Devil Island base camp is almost purely preparation for the next trip. Older boys paddle as far as James Bay in each six- to seven-week session. It is felt that the hardships of such a life introduce the boys to hard work, co-operation, and a sense of pride

Campers at Camp Keewaydin.

in overcoming problems.

In 1910 Camp Ojibway was established on Devil Island as a place for families and friends of Keewaydin campers to stay.

Camp Temagami was founded in 1903 by Upper Canada College physical education instructor A.L. Cochrane on two islands in the South Arm. For several years accommodations were in tents, then a large dining hall was built and gradually other buildings were added. Patrons were Canadian, as opposed to the exclusively American campers at Keewaydin, with many of them coming, naturally enough, from Upper Canada College. Cochrane promoted a recreational experience rather than the more military lifestyle of Keewaydin. Campers took the English Royal Life Saving Society course, and social effectiveness, gentlemanly conduct, and good citizenship were stressed. When Camp Accouchiching to the south closed down, it was purchased by Camp Temagami and opened as a girls' camp renamed Camp Metagami.

Changes in family vacation patterns and rising costs forced both camps to close in the early 1970s. The properties are now private cottages.

The largest youth camp on the lake is Camp Wabikon on Temagami Island. Wabikon, which means "little white flower" in Ojibwa, was from ancient times the summer meeting place of the native people. Not far from the property are the remains of the original Hudson's Bay Company post and an Ojibwa cemetery. It was an adult camp in 1925 when Grey Owl worked there. After the Second World War, it became the first co-educational camp on Lake Temagami, and today, each three-week session hosts up to 150 campers attended by 50 staff members.

All campers count among their souvenirs the lifelong friendships forged in a summer of shared experiences and a myriad of happy memories. Every camp forms its own traditions, and these figure stongly in the memories of the campers. There are fishing derbies — Camp Chimo (which closed in 1974) one summer gave top honours for a 9.5-kilogram lake trout and a 5.4-kilogram pickerel — and regattas featuring decorated boats and canoes and events such as "gunny-bobbing," in which a canoe is propelled forward by someone standing on the gunwales and bouncing up and down by bending their knees. Bathing suits are *de rigueur* for this event.

The campers at Camp Pays d'en Haut on Island 583 in the South-West Arm eschewed commercialism to make their own trophies. An old pair of disreputable shorts honours those who have made the Sturgeon River trip; animal skins and even worn-out boots

record other adventures. A pair of tattered snowshoes converted to giant fly swatters bears tongue-in-cheek testimony to the rigours of the trail. The walls hold sun-bleached photos dating to the camp's beginnings in 1930, photos of proud, earnest young men who found friends for life as they shared trips. The bow of a canoe juts out from one wall, souvenir of a faithful craft now relegated to memories.

The Pays d'en Haut Elementary Wilderness Certificate can only be earned by those with a good grounding in canoe and tripping skills, but Gord Deeks, a leader at Pays d'en Haut, maintains no canoe-tripping is satisfy-

ing until one gets away from all signs of civilization. The Temagami area, he says, is the last wilderness still offering relatively easy access from southern centres.

Those camp buildings that have managed to avoid being destroyed by fire often delight the senses with their rustic charm. The elegant log lodge at Wanapitei, for example, will probably be designated a heritage site. There are claims that it is the oldest log building in the Temagami area. Founded in 1931 on the site of Father Paradis's settlement at Sandy Inlet in the North Arm, Wanapitei specialized in canoe-tripping and recreation. Today, its long sandy beach is a great drawing card for families and small conference groups.

The green-stained buildings of Camp Pays d'en Haut are dwarfed by towering pines. A small wooden water tower is ballasted by large rocks, and windows on cabins are held open by ingenious rope-and-pulley devices.

The buildings at Camp Eucaroma, on the northeast side of Temagami Island, were constructed of lumber and logs cut and milled on site and lugged up a hillside. The first building was a kitchen with an Adam Hall stove big enough to cook six pies at once. Next came a dining room with a huge boulder fireplace. Cabins came later, after the log lodge. There was an icehouse where sawdust over 45-kilogram blocks of ice preserved perishables, and a root cellar for fresh vegetables. The brown-and-white-checkered pump house became a local landmark.

The name *Eucaroma* was created from the initials of the daughters of the camp's founders. One of those daughters was married in the mission church on Bear Island in 1938 by a priest who came from North Bay for the event. He was very nervous: not only was the couple the first non-native couple to be married there, but he had just had his first plane ride, his first power-boat ride, and he was about to perform his first wedding! The reception was held across the lake in the lodge at Eucaroma. That lodge is still there, but the camp's name is now Camp Adanac.

Camper graffiti at Camp Wabikon. Lynne Birnie

There are many, many camps on Lake Temagami, catering to every aspect of the market. There are also more resorts and inns than it is possible to mention here. There are motels, hotels, housekeeping cabins, and fishing camps. For those who prefer to plan their own wilderness holiday, there are outfitters. For example, just north of Temagami, Smoothwater Wilderness Outfitters excels in providing supplies and information for canoeists and other outdoors enthusiasts, groups or solo travellers. Owner Hap Wilson's book on canoe routes is first-rate.

The variety of camps, lodges, and resorts on Lake Temagami run the gamut of all tastes, and yet the huge lake is never crowded. The wilderness is still Temagami's most valuable commodity.   •

The sheltered anchorage at
Finlayson Park.
MNR

Precious Resources

Steam and electric trains seen together at Cobalt in this 1910 photo. Today the pillars remain but the trains are just a memory.   OA S12707

TEMAGAMI'S plentiful natural gifts would seem to leave the area open to exploitation. Certainly the obvious beauty of the area makes tourism a continuing resource. The lake has plentiful fish, and, in fact, there was a commercial fishery earlier in the century, but its output was minimal. The area's most clearly exploitable — and most controversial — resources are minerals and timber.

Until the 1950s all successful mining had been done to the north, around Cobalt, Porcupine, and Kirkland Lake, and to the west, in Sudbury. Although the presence of minerals in Temagami had been known for a hundred years, all prospects either failed at the exploration stage or were small mines which failed through lack of ore or inadequate exploration. Robert Bell and A.E. Barlow, field men with the Geological Survey of Canada, had noted in 1901 several places "where the compass was much affected," and there was sporadic activity from then until 1960, much of it centred in Strathy Township, due south of Temagami and bisected by Highway 11. Gold, silver, and arsenic showed in values that did not justify further work.

Mining firms have had difficulty convincing governments to allow them to mine in parks and near beauty spots. Both parties might do well to examine Copperfields, a rich copper property on Temagami

Island that was worked for 17 years without harming the place's natural beauty. Normal Keevil and his associates even pinpointed the exact location of Copperfields without any surface drilling.

Normal Keevil went from a Saskatchewan farm background to a science education and finally to the University of Toronto, where in 1937 he became the

Arthur Stevens' store, Temagami, 1909.

first professor in the relatively new field of geophysics. Following the war, Keevil and his associates ran the first aeromagnetic surveys in the Temagami area for a number of years before confirming with some surface drilling the existence of the largest body of copper ore ever found in Canada. But the deposit was located on Temagami Island, a prime resort area, and there was no road access to the property. Nonetheless, the acquisition of claims to the area went ahead and plans were formed to obtain the rich copper ore.

The mine would not be noticeable from the lake, for it would be centred in a basin, and surrounding trees would be left standing to further mask mining activity. A smelter would not be required; truckloads of ore could be barged to a landing place to be driven to Noranda for processing. The company proposed to bear the half-million-dollar cost of building a road from the lake to Highway 11.

Predictably, cottage and resort owners were not keen on any mining activity on the lake, but the province gave permission for the venture to proceed and the mine was opened in 1954. The ore taken from the open pits was so rich that initial operations were financed from only the first three months of operation. In its lifespan the mine produced nearly a half a million kilograms of copper as well as some gold, silver, and platinum, for a total value of $33 million. Best of all for Temagami, 320 persons were employed year-round for 17 years.

When the property closed in 1972, the open pits were filled and all buildings except the housing were removed. The area was landscaped and replanted. Dr. Keevil had proposed that a major resort be built in the mine's place, but the province refused. Nonetheless, users of Lake Temagami were able to enjoy the benefits brought to the area by a good corporate neighbour. One benefit was the mine road. Renamed the Access Road, it eliminated a lengthy boat trip down the North-East Arm for resort guests and cottage owners. Another was the arrival of electricity and the telephone to the lake.

Dan O'Connor, the local entrepreneur who founded the Boat Line and opened the Halfway House, had iron claims north of Temagami. In 1902 geologist William Miller, the man who had confirmed the existence of the Cobalt deposits, did an exhaustive survey there which indicated a large ore body. There were technical problems, but by 1913 German interests had optioned the property. Their involvement came to an end with the advent of the Second World War. Interest waned for 30 years as supplies of iron were plentiful elsewhere, particularly in the United States, and it wasn't until 1944 that several companies began once again to explore the property. Technology in the pelletizing process of refining ore had developed in the intervening years,

In 1934 this hotel was a popular spot in Temagami. Verla Pacey

land near the former townsite of Goward, an old lumber mill, would become a model satellite suburb of Temagami. By 1987 the Sherman had shipped 19 million metric tons of iron pellets and there were reserves for at least eight years left. Things looked rosy for the Sherman Mine and for Temagami.

But the Sherman and its sister plant, the Adams Mine of Kirkland Lake, closed in March 1990. Costs had escalated and only giant-sized properties could compete with the South American iron which was being bought and shipped to Canada for less than it would cost to produce at either of the two northern Ontario mines. The mines announced liberal severance packages and closing arrangements with the communities, and the government announced grants to enable Temagami to enhance its tourist potential and to look for smaller, more diversified companies. Eventually there will be an

and when in 1958 a natural gas pipeline reached Temiskaming, offering a reliable efficient fuel supply, the Sherman Mine could become a reality. Work started on the construction of the mine in 1964. First a road was built to connect it with the main highway just past the Milne lumber mill. The Ontario Northland ran a spur line to the property and purchased special covered cars to ship the pellets to Hamilton. Vast quantities of rock and overburden were removed from the site and from what would become the three open pits in the three years of construction before the mine opened. On start-up day it was calculated that the concentrating plant, pellet plant, and mining equipment had cost $40 million.

Dofasco of Hamilton owned the mine, which eventually covered 3,000 hectares and employed 320 workers, and it was managed by Cliffs of Canada. The need for additional workers in the district meant that

The Temagami Grill and General Store. J. R. Stevens

airport at the former mine site and there are plans for a resort complex close to Temagami, but times are hard economically and the loss of the Sherman Mine has not been easy for the area to take.

There has been commercial logging in the Temagami district ever since the coming of the railway. Recently, the focus on Temagami in newspaper articles has given the impression that the white and the red pines are the predominant tree species in the area forests. Actually this is a mixed forest region. Lowlands and swamps have black spruce, tamarack, and white cedar, and pines are found in upland country. The white pine grows with white birch, white spruce (both of which are normally as abundant as the pine), balsam fir, and aspen species. Red pines grow alongside jack pines on bluffs and along ridges with dry, sandy, or rocky soil. There are also hardwoods such as yellow birch and sugar maple scattered thinly throughout. Pines are found across Canada, but the eastern varieties don't grow as large as those in British Columbia which have the benefits of plentiful rainfall and mild winters. Left alone in ideal conditions their lifespan covers hundreds of years. To the forest industry, the bottom line is that a white pine can provide up to 16 cubic metres of timber and a red pine may offer up to 12.5 cubic metres. In recent years, foresters have spent more time studying pines than any other species. They hope to produce seed varieties that will mature to harvest faster than the current cycle of about a hundred years.

Canadians have nostalgic visions of the great pine forests of the past. The pines conjure up images of rafting, camp life and honest toil. In 1871 John A. MacDonald, alarmed at the volume of timber he saw rafting down the Ottawa River, wondered how the industry could be regulated and set in motion an act, passed seven years later, "To Preserve the Forests from Destruction." Measures, including the appointment of the first fire rangers, were taken to protect Algonquin Park in the

*Temagami fire rangers pose for a photograph
in the late 1920s.*

1880s. When in 1895 the Dominion Bureau of Statistics warned that without care Canada would cease to be a wood-exporting nation, Ontario was moved to pass the Forest Reserves Act, which also banned fishing and hunting in designated areas.

The Temagami Forest Reserve was set up in 1901 to safeguard what later came to be close to 15,500 square hectares of trees for future use by the forest industry. Included in this vast area, far more land than the Temagami district itself encompassed, was the largest stand of red and white pine left in Canada. Later the Mississauga, Nipigon, and Quetico reserves were added, making Ontario the North American leader in forest management. With this legislation, the province felt it had established a perpetual supply of timber, but the concept was not well developed and over the years successive governments made exceptions to the original area and failed to enforce regulations uniformly. Crown Timber Regulations were made to control timber permit holders, but there was insufficient staff to police them. Timber permit holders were those companies given permission to log in the reserve. The Milne Lumber Company, for example, was given permission to cut timber along the railway right-of-way. Only when public outcry surfaced over the huge revenues derived from cutting permits was the province forced to regulate the lumber trade seriously.

A chief ranger was stationed at Bear Island in 1906 to supervise about 50 fire rangers spread throughout the reserve. Later the officer moved to Forestry Island in Portage Bay, and by 1910 he supervised close to half the provincial complement. The rangers did a splendid job of fire control, but no one realized then that fire is an essential factor in the life cycle of healthy pine forests.

A huge fire in Cassells Township north of Temagami in 1923 necessitated the salvage of millions of board feet of pine. The Temagami Timber Company was formed to take the timber, and the village of Goward at the Net Narrows Bridge grew to accommodate its workers. The mill at Goward survived for years on fire cull and later on over-mature lumber. The process of whittling down the reserve's timber had begun. Fire-patrol pilots of the Provincial Air Service, which had a base on Lake Temagami by 1930, could observe how much logging activity went on in spring and fall when tourists and cottagers were not there to be disturbed by it.

Towards the end of the Second World War, pilot Carl Crossley of the Provincial Air Service led experiments in water-bombing on Lake Temagami which would have great significance for forest-fire fighting around the world. When a snorkel device failed to provide sufficient pressure to fill the barrels on planes, they were filled using a fire pump. Even with a limited barrel capacity, it was found, an aircraft could extinguish a small blaze. Further experiments established that floats under the plane could be used to contain the water. Each float held 208 litres and the water could be scooped up while the plane taxied across the lake. The water could be jettisoned in nine seconds: the world's first aerial fire tanker was in operation.

As time passed, Temagami area mills experienced difficulty in obtaining further cutting permits from the province. Goward closed in 1965, Milne kept open by utilizing wood chips and careful waste management. The problem came to a head in the late 1980s when Ontario began to extend the Red Squirrel Road to access old-growth pine and found it had a big environmental fight on its hands. The Temagami Indian band blockaded the road, followed by the Temagami Wilderness Society, and huge policing costs were incurred to keep the peace. The road was eventually completed, but the lesson came through clearly: all future use of wilderness areas would be monitored carefully by public interest groups. The Temagami Advisory Council, a citizen's group appointed by the province, now monitors all resource planning, and their public meetings allow environmental input.

The Ministry of Natural Resources says they have located 26,000 hectares of pines over 120 years old within the Temagami forest. The dominant species in that forest now has become the black spruce. White pine has slipped to sixth most dominant and red pine to seventh of the eight counted varieties of standing trees. The decline in pine results from selective logging and from the suppression of fire. Mature and over-mature trees have to be cut to invigorate the land and provide opportunities for new growth, and periodic forest fires provide a seed bed for pines. To restore the forest, the ministry has planted 160,000 seedlings since 1980, and they intend to plant two million more in the last decade of the century. Over 100,000 hectares of park land have been set aside in the district, including three new waterway parks, and 225 kilometres of popular canoe routes have been protected.

The loggers have been pitted against the environmentalists in Temagami, but the industry shares a stake in protecting the forest and renewing the trees. Economic considerations as well as recreational interests have made the province aware of the need to revitalize pine forests, and the outcome seems certain to have all the elements of a typical Canadian compromise. The forest *will* be developed but at the same time aesthetic values *will* be protected.

Meanwhile, there is a glimmer of good news for the economic life of Temagami in the lifting of the native peoples' land caution on part of the land to allow prospecting. The dispute still awaits a court ruling and nothing will be settled without a legal decision, but renewed activity offers new hope.

Some lessons have been learned. Resource-based industries must respect the rights of recreational land users, who, on the other hand, must realize that there is a place for development of precious resources, if the land is not scarred and if that development can be sustained. •

Informed Action

An enchanting view of Lake Temagami.　　J. R. Stevens

THE poet Archibald Lampman loved the Temagami area and canoed here often. The region's beauty moved him to write:

Far in the Northwest beyond the lines
That turn the rivers eastward to the sea,
Set with a thousand islands, crowned with pines,
Lies the deep water, wild Temagami.
Wild for the hunter's roving and the use
Of trappers in its dark and trackless vales,
And the weird magic of Old Indian tales.
All day with steady paddles toward the west
Our heavy-laden long-canoe we pressed,
All day we saw the thunder-travelled sky
Purpled with storm in many a trailing tress,
And saw at eve the broken sunset die
In crimson on the silent wilderness.

Wilson MacDonald, another poet, visited the lake more than 50 years after Lampman and saluted it in his poem, "Singing Words":

Temiscaming has a singing sound
　　Like pine trees sweet and low.
Paris and Rome are iron words:
　　They speak but they do not flow.
Boston is as cold as Arctic ice,
　　Moscow's abrupt yet strong.
But when you have said, "Temagami,"
　　You feel you have sung a song.

First-time visitors to Temagami find themselves becoming possessive about the lake. How much stronger is the feeling of ownership felt by cottagers who have had family ties with Lake Temagami for

many years — ownership not so much of the land and water as of the peace and solitude the lonely waterway brings. Columnist Don Curry has written, "You don't own the land. In winter the elements own it and in summer the mosquitoes." But all who are struck by its beauty want to preserve the waters of Temagami for future generations.

Former Ontario Premier David Peterson admitted that one of the most difficult questions he ever had to face in politics was that of land use of the territory from the Lady Evelyn–Smoothwater Wilderness Park down to the southern tip of Lake Temagami, an area half the size of Prince Edward Island. The dissension caused by that question brought about some new action groups, one of which was the Temagami Wilderness Society. Members believe that the stands of old-growth pine in Temagami are part of our heritage and can never be replaced. The society also seeks to preserve the scenery, the rare wildlife concentrated in the area, and the archaeological sites, many of which have not yet been explored, or perhaps even discovered. Through broadsheets and advertisements, members and the public are kept informed of any initiatives which impact upon the Temagami forest. Government action thought to be detrimental to the land is challenged in the courts. The organization is funded by both individual and corporate donors. Efforts have drawn attention at the international level — the Swiss-based International Union for the Conservation of Nature has declared the old-growth pine stands of Temagami to be an endangered area.

Northcare takes a different tack from the Wilderness Society. This group sponsors multiple uses of Crown lands and waters. Northcare represents those who wish to protect the environment but who also believe that the forest is a renewable resource, sustainable through proper cutting methods and planting. Recreation is just one of the possible uses for the land and waters. Among Northcare supporters are individuals, corporations, and chambers of commerce. The Temagami

A canoeist on a portage path.
Gary McGuffin

Andy Stevens

Women's Action Group has a similar focus with a special emphasis on the retention of jobs in the area.

The Temagami Lakes Association, formed during the early 1930s, is now more than 600 members strong. The constitution of the association supports the preservation of the recreational and aesthetic values of the region and the position of the Indian people, their land claims, and their view that certain lands are sacred. The TLA is committed to the health, safety, and welfare of its members so that they may live in harmony with the land and waters. There is an annual directory of all members, and quarterly issues of the *Temagami Times*, a mixture of information, articles on nature and history and current concerns, are sent out. There is a mail and message service, a radio monitor, archives and a museum, a library, and a twice-a-year property check.

The headquarters building of the TLA sits at the end of the Access Road with windows overlooking the lake. A browse through the museum unearths a nice jumble of artifacts: a letter from a guide during the Depression years asking his employer for a salary of $25 a month and the reply from his employer refusing his request but telling him to do his job well; old motors and implements (some with plaintive requests as to their function); memories of boats of the past — a lifebelt from the *Aubrey Cousins V.C.*; and the "Domesday Book," showing all land leases on the lake since 1906. Pictures of Grey Owl hang next to a 1901 clipping from *The Globe and Mail* stating the new forest reserve will be free, "for posterity has no political influence." Upstairs, two students answer telephones and radios and serve in the shop. Tim Gooderham, the association's executive secretary and an articulate supporter of the lake he has visited since the late 1930s, emphasizes that

A mother grebe swims by with her young.

Gary McGuffin

the TLA was always pro-active. Indeed, they won the original skyline reserve more than 50 years ago.

The loon is the symbol of the Temagami Lakes Association, and the big bird with the striking black-and-white plumage, the legendary necklace, and the long pointed bill makes its home on Lake Temagami in large numbers. A recent count showed 221 adults. Considered, along with the grebe, to be one of the world's most ancient bird species, the loon can live up to 20 years. They can stay underwater for three minutes and can fish as deep as 21 metres. Loons' short wingspans and set-back legs make it difficult for them to launch their 4-kilogram bodies into the air, but once aloft they can reach speeds of over 100 kilometres per hour. Acid rain, pollution and human expansion have decimated the loon population, and volunteers across the country report on sightings in support of studies to preserve it.

No one who has seen a loon carrying its young on its back, or heard its lonesome yodels and wails at night or in the early morning mist, can fail to be touched by this distinctive bird. Long may it grace Lake Temagami with its mirthless laugh and eerie wolf-like howl.

Human anglers compete with the loon for certain species of fish in the lake. Temagami has the most sought-after northern game fish: yellow pickerel or walleye, lake trout, and at least 20 other varieties. The surrounding bush is filled with numerous species of mushrooms, ferns, flowers, and shrubs. More than 30 species of birds frequent the area, including the rare golden eagle. Mammals range from the ordinary cottontail to moose, marten, river otters, and eastern cougars.

Andy Stevens

If you wish to know more about the organizations mentioned or about others which relate to Temagami, contact them at the following addresses:

Association of Youth Camps on Temagami Lake
7 Engleburn Place, Peterborough, Ontario, K9H 1C4

Canadian Lakes Loon Survey
Long Point Bird Observatory, Box 160, Port Rowan, Ontario, N0E 1M0

Temagami Chamber of Commerce
Box 57, Temagami, Ontario, P0H 2H0

Northcare
(Northern Community Advocates for Resource Equity)
Box 1405, North Bay, Ontario, P1B 8K6

Lady Evelyn Owners and Users Association
Box 100, Latchford, Ontario, P0J 1N0

Temagami Lakes Association
(winter) Box 842, North Bay, Ontario, P1B 8K1;
(summer) Box 129, Temagami, Ontario, P0H 2H0

Temagami Tourist Operators Association
Group Box 13, Temagami, Ontario, P0H 2H0

Earthroots
401 Richmond St. W., Toronto, Ontario M5V 3A8

Temagami Women's Action Group
Group Box 52, Temagami, Ontario, P0H 2H0

Teme-Augama Anishnabai
Bear Island, Lake Temagami, Ontario, P0H 1C0

Temagami Wilderness Fund
Box 842, North Bay, Ontario P1B 8K1

Selected Bibliography

BOOKS

Anahareo. *Devil in Deerskins*. Toronto: New Press, 1972.

Back, B. *The Keewaydin Way*. Temagami: Keewaydin Camps Ltd., 1983.

Barnes, M. *Fortunes in the Ground*. Erin: The Boston Mills Press, 1986.

———. *Link with a Lonely Land*. Erin: The Boston Mills Press, 1985.

———. *Killer in the Bush*. Erin: The Boston Mills, Press, 1987.

Cassidy, G. *Arrow North*. Cobalt: Highway, 1976.

Conway, T. *Archaeology in Northeastern Ontario*, Toronto: Ministry of Culture and Citizenship, 1981.

Dickson, L. *Wilderness Man*. Toronto: Macmillan, 1973.

Grey Owl. *Men of the Last Frontier*. Toronto: Macmillan, 1931.

———. *Tales of an Empty Cabin*. Toronto: Macmillan, 1931.

A History of the Sudbury Forest District. Toronto: Department of Lands and Forests, 1967.

Hodgins, B. *Paradis of Temagami*. Cobalt: Highway, 1976.

———. *The Temagami Experience*. Toronto: University of Toronto, 1974.

Lampman, A. The Peoms of Archibald Lampman. Toronto: University of Toronto, 1947.

MacDonald, W. *Armand Dussault and Other Poems*. Toronto: Macmillan, 1946.

Mackay, D. *Heritage Lost: The Crisis in Canada's Forests*. Toronto, Macmillan, 1985.

Mitchell, E. *Fort Timiskaming and the Fur Trade*. Toronto: University of Toronto, 1977.

Nelles, H. V. *The Politics of Development*. Toronto: Macmillan, 1974.

Pain, S. A. *The Way North*. Toronto: Ryerson, 1964.

Pink, H. *King of the Woodsmen*. London: Macmillan, 1940.

Scholl, J. *Ontario Since 1867*. Toronto: McClelland and Stewart, 1978.

Smith, D. *Long Lance*. Toronto: Macmillan, 1982.

Theriault, M. *Moose to Moccasins*. North Bay: private, 1985.

Tucker A. *Steam into Wilderness*. Toronto: Fitzhenry and Whiteside, 1978.

Wilson, H. *Temagami Canoe Routes*. Temagami: Ministry of Natural Resources, 1984.

West, B. *The Firebirds*. Toronto: Queen's Printer, 1974.

Warman, C. *Weiga of Temagami*. Toronto: McLeod and Allen, 1908.

PAMPHLETS, PAPERS AND ARTICLES

Day, R., Carter, J. *Interim Research on the Ecology and Silviculture of Late Successional White and Red Pine Forest*. Thunder Bay: Lakehead University, 1989.

Grey Owl. "Who Will Repay?" *Canadian Forest and Outdoors*. March, 1931.

Guppy, E. *Diary 1890–1940*. Temagami: private, 1940.

Helleiner, F. "Sandy Inlet: Peace in a Popular Wilderness." *Canadian Geographical Journal*, Feb.-Mar., 1977.

Mitcham, A. "Reminiscences of Grey Owl's Daughter." *Northward Journal*, vol. 13, 1979.

Moise, B. "Temagami: A Wilderness Under Siege." *Canadian Geographical Journal*, Feb.-Mar., 1989.

News, T. *Rocking Chair News*. Temagami: private, 1987.

Stevens, W. *Characteristics of Eastern White Pine and Red Pine*. Petawawa: Department of the Environment, 1978.

Temagami Centennial Booklet. Temagami: Centennial Committee, 1967.

The Author

MICHAEL Barnes has lived most of his life in Northern Ontario. Four of his books about Northern Ontario are *Link with a Lonely Land* (the Temiskaming & Northern Ontario Railway), *Fortunes in the Ground* (the famous mining camps), *Killer in the Bush* (the great forest fires), *Polar Bear Express Country* (the train to the arctic tidewater and the places it serves). One of his most recent books is *Policing Ontario — The OPP Today*. All were published by The Boston Mills Press.

The author makes his home at Round Lake, not far from Kirkland Lake. He is currently researching a new book, *Gold in Ontario*.

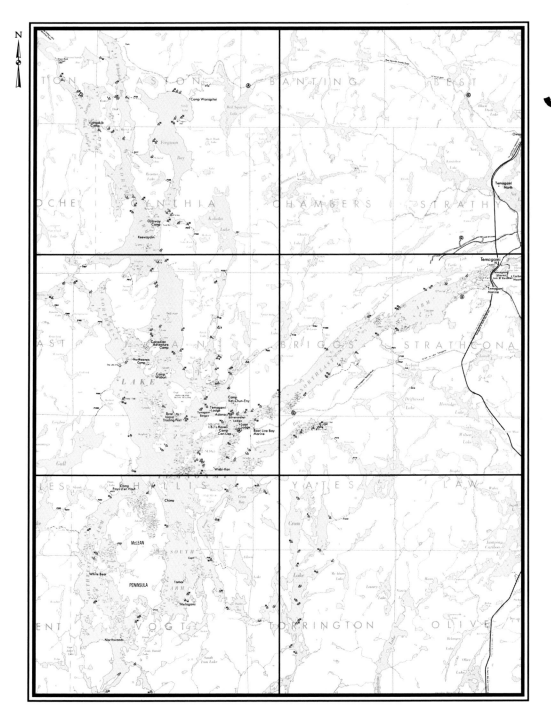

Ontario's Family
Wilderness Adventure

ISLANDS IN
LAKE TEMAGAMI
DISTRICT OF NIPISSING

LEGEND

ACCESS POINT . . . . (A)

WASTE DISPOSAL SITE . . . . (G)

CAMPSITE . . . . △

PORTAGE (length in metres) *P119*

CAMPSITE RATING: based on a maximum number of 2-men tent sites available per campsite

TENT SITES	RATING
1-2	S-small
3-5	M-medium
6 and up	L-large

One Inch equals One Mile

This map is available at retail outlets and lodges throughout the Temagami area.

To order by mail, contact:
Susan Plumstead, Box 421, Temagami,
Ontario P0H 2H0   (705) 569-2921

Page 96 photo:
Jack L. Goodman

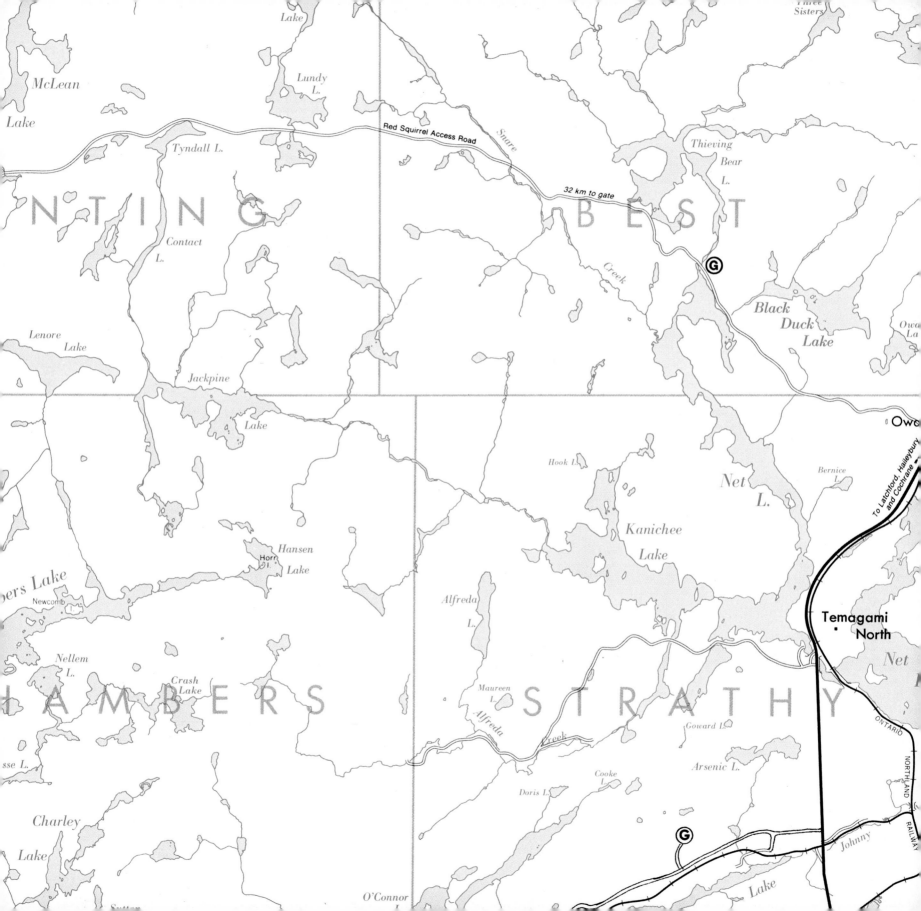

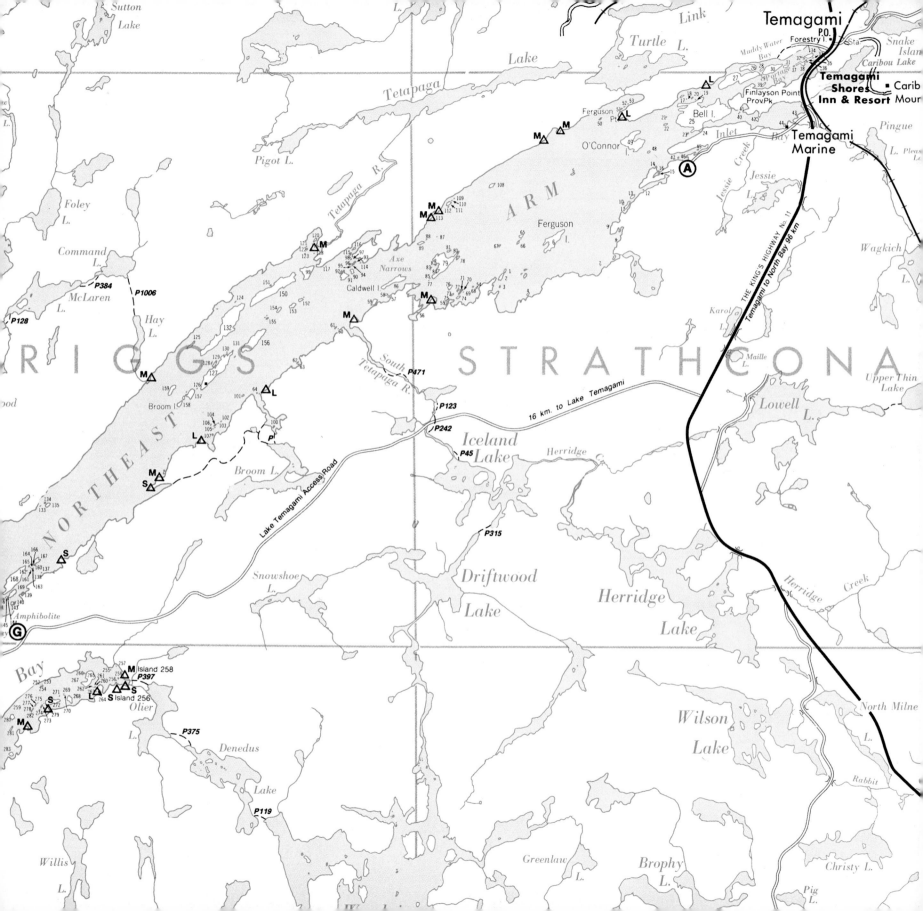

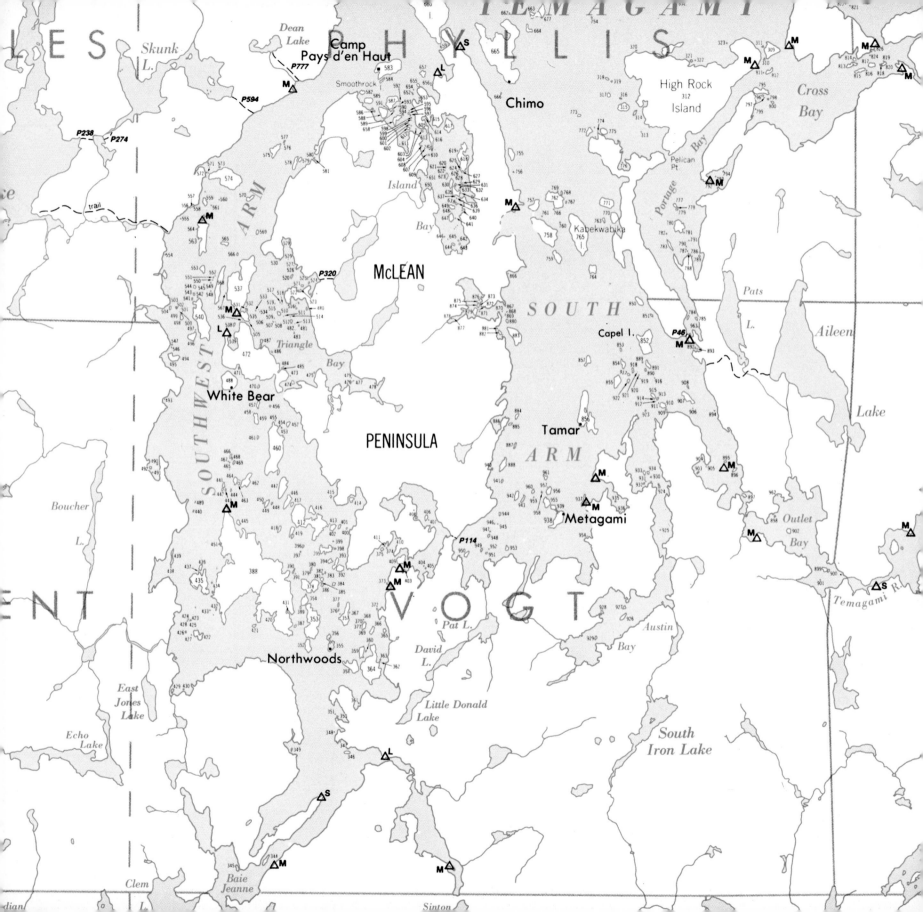

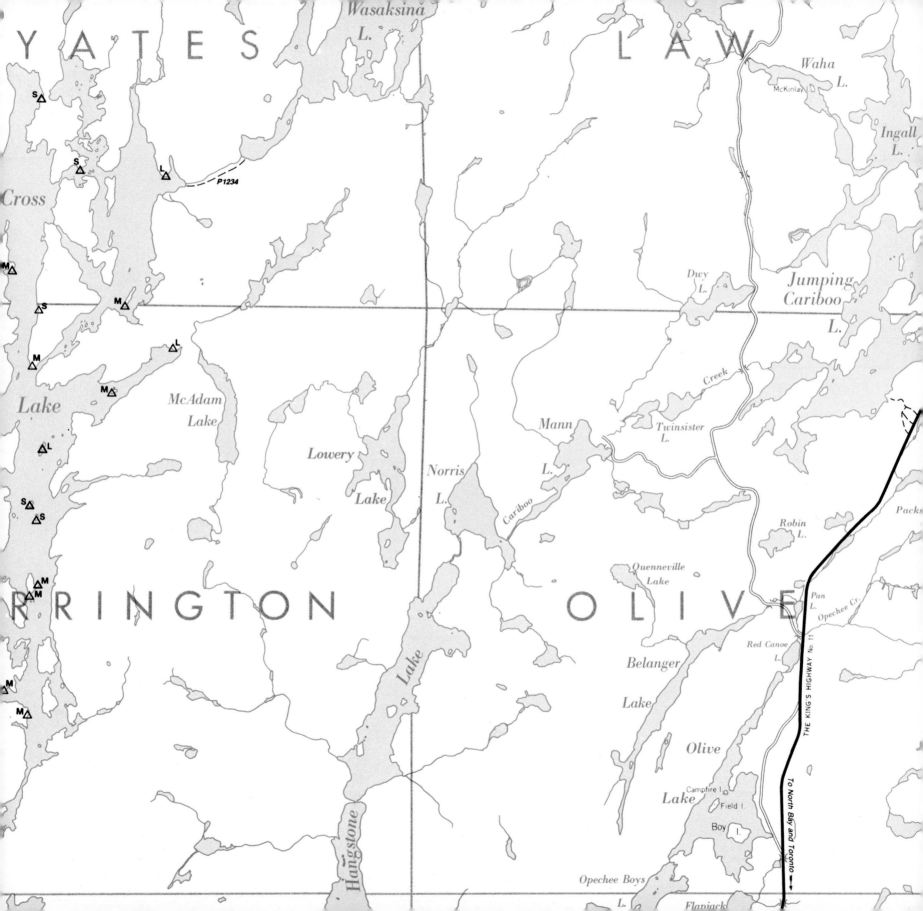

Y A T E S

Wasaksina L.

L A W

Waha L.

McKinlay I.

Ingall L.

S

S

L

P1234

Cross

M

M

S

M

L

Lake

M

M

L

S

S

M
M
M

R R I N G T O N

M

M

McAdam Lake

Lowery Lake

Norris L.

Cariboo

Mann L.

Dwy L.

Jumping Cariboo L.

Creek

Twinsister L.

Robin L.

Quenneville Lake

O L I V E

Pan L.

Opechee Cr.

Packs

Red Canoe L.

THE KING'S HIGHWAY No. 11

Belanger Lake

Olive

Lake

Campfire I.

Field I.

Boy I.

Hangstone

Opechee Boys

Flapjack

To North Bay and Toronto